Author of Push Your Way into A Happy Relationship

Addressing
Needs, Wants, & Desires
in a Healthy Relationship!

Harrison S. Mungal. PhD, PsyD

Addressing Needs, Wants, & Desires
in a Healthy Relationship!

Copyright © Harrison S. Mungal

All rights reserved. Neither this publication nor any part of this publication may be reproduced or transmitted in any form or by any means, electronic or mechanical, including photocopying, recording or any information storage and retrieval system, without permission in writing from the author.

Contact author via
info@agetoage.ca
www.agetoage.ca
www.harrisonmungal.com
www.harrisonmungalbooks.com
Facebook: Harrison Mungal
Twitter: AgeToAgeInc1
LinkedIn: Harrison Mungal, Ph.D., PsyD
YouTube: Harrison Mungal
Phone: 905-533-1334

ABOUT *the* AUTHOR

With an extensive background in clinical psychology, Harrison is deeply committed to enhancing the lives of those he counsels. His academic credentials are impressive, boasting dual doctoral degrees in Clinical Psychology and Philosophy in Social Work and two master's degrees in Social Work and Counselling. He also holds a Bachelor's degree in Theology. His areas of expertise encompass mental health, addiction, marital and relationship, family dynamics, and parenting issues.

Recognized as a leading authority in cognitive therapy, Harrison is a sought-after presenter at workshops. His multifaceted role allows him to assist individuals, couples, families, and corporations. Harrison, a global public speaker, has addressed audiences in over 42 countries at various conferences, seminars, and public events. His reach extends to radio and television appearances and he has authored over 30 books. He is widely respected for his profound insights, as well as his engaging sense of humour and enthusiasm for subjects like mental health, addictions, relationships, and parenting.

Harrison's approach to his work is both inventive and grounded in scientific principles. This unique methodology has earned him a sterling reputation, along with multiple awards and accolades from an array of institutions, including law enforcement agencies, municipal governments, community leaders, and corporate executives. He offers training and consultations to a diverse range of community partners, including medical professionals, social workers, first responders, law enforcement officials, and senior management teams.

An active participant in cognitive research, Harrison has led several groundbreaking studies aimed at aiding people with mental health issues like addiction, psychosis, anxiety, and depression. Among these studies are explorations into music therapy for schizophrenia, vaccination protocols for young children, and the role of substance abuse in the food service industry. His work on Thought Developmental Practice (TDP) has been particularly notable for providing alternative treatments for conditions like substance abuse, anxiety, PTSD, and depression under Dr. David Koczerginski, a chief psychiatrist.

With over two decades of professional experience, Harrison has worked with a broad and diverse range of populations. His experience encompasses 17 years in the mental health and psychiatry fields and more than a decade as a practicing clinical psychotherapist. He has provided services to a myriad of communities, including those affected by Acquired Brain Injuries, refugees, victims of warfare, and individuals in crisis across various settings, which include collaborations with police forces, hospitals, community agencies, and inpatient mental health facilities.

In terms of therapeutic approaches, Harrison is well-versed in a wide array of evidence-based treatments. These include, but are not limited to, Cognitive Behavioral Therapy (CBT), Cognitive Processing Therapy (CPT), Dialectical Behavioral Therapy (DBT), and Acceptance and Commitment Therapy (ACT). He is also skilled in Interpersonal Therapy (IPT), Motivational Interviewing Techniques, Grounding Techniques, and various other specialized forms of treatment, such as Humanistic Experiential Therapy and Psychodynamic Therapy.

Author: Harrison S. Mungal.

TABLE of CONTENT

ABOUT THE AUTHOR.. 3
INTRODUCTION 11
    WHAT WILL YOU GAIN? .... **Error! Bookmark not defined.**
PURPOSE AND VALUE 15
    WHAT IS THE PURPOSE OF A RELATIONSHIP? 17
    WHY DO WE DESIRE OR WANT TO BE IN A
    RELATIONSHIP?.. 18
    WHAT WE CAN GIVE AND NOT WHAT WE CAN GET 18
    WHAT ARE WE WILLING TO GIVE UP AND COMPROMISE?
    19
    SOME OBSTACLES THAT CAN BECOME PROBLEMS IN A
    RELATIONSHIP?.. 20
    WHAT ARE EXPECTATIONS BROUGHT INTO
    RELATIONSHIPS? 21
    WHAT GIVES VALUE TO RELATIONSHIPS?............................ 22
    WHY THE NEED TO RECOGNIZE VALUE AND WORTH IN
    A RELATIONSHIP? 23
    WHY DO WE NEED TO EXPLORE OUR SELF-WORTH AND
    SELF-VALUE?... 24

- HOW DO YOU IDENTIFY WORTH AND VALUE IN A RELATIONSHIP? ... 24
- HOW DO WE BRING OUT THE VALUE AND WORTH IN A RELATIONSHIP? ... 25
- WHY DO WE NEED TO APPRECIATE SKILLS, KNOWLEDGE, AND EXPERIENCE? ... 26
- TOOLS TO BUILD PURPOSE AND VALUE ... 28

INVESTMENT ... 29
- WHAT DOES IT MEAN TO INVEST IN A RELATIONSHIP? ... 31
- WHY SHOULD A RELATIONSHIP BE CONSIDERED A BUSINESS? ... 32
- ARE COUPLES CONSIDERED PARTNERS IN THE BUSINESS OF A RELATIONSHIP? ... 33
- HOW DO WE AVOID INTIMATIONS? ... 34
- HOW DO WE IDENTIFY THE NEED TO GROW THE RELATIONSHIP? ... 35
- TOOLS TO KEEP INVESTING IN THE RELATIONSHIP ... 36

UNDERSTANDING ... 38
- UNDERSTANDING EACH OTHER'S STRENGTHS ... 40
- UNDERSTANDING PERSONALITY AND CHARACTERS ... 41
- ADDRESSING INSECURITIES, LACK OF CONFIDENCE, AND LOW SELF-ESTEEM ... 42
- MISTAKES, PAST ADVERSE HISTORY, BAD HABITS, AND WRONGDOING ... 45
- ACCEPTING IMPERFECTIONS, FLAWS, AND WEAKNESSES ... 46
- UNDERSTANDING OPINIONS AND PERCEPTIONS ... 47
- UNDERSTANDING MENTAL HEALTH, INCLUDING OCD AND PERFECTIONISM ... 48
- UNDERSTANDING ORGANIC-RELATED ISSUES ... 49

- UNDERSTANDING BAD HABITS, ADDICTIONS, AND BEHAVIOURS 50
- UNDERSTANDING PERSONALITY DISORDERS AND NARCISSISTIC TRAITS 51
- UNDERSTANDING BOUNDARIES AND LIMITATIONS 52
- CREATE NEW MEMORY CARDS 54
- TOOLS TO BUILD YOURSELF AND OTHERS 55

SOME MEN THINK DIFFERENTLY 56
- HOW DO SOME MEN THINK DIFFERENTLY THAN SOME WOMEN? 58
- WHAT DOES THE BRAIN HAVE TO SAY ABOUT THIS? 59
- HOW DO SOME MEN REACT TO EMOTIONS? 61
- WHY SOME WOMEN CAN BE MORE EMOTIONAL THAN SOME MEN? 62
- HOW TO BALANCE THE THREE MINDS? 64
- BODY LANGUAGE AND NON-VERBAL COMMUNICATION 66
- ROLES AND RESPONSIBILITIES 67

WANTS AND NEEDS 70
- WHAT IS THE DIFFERENCE BETWEEN A NEED AND A WANT? 72
- WHAT IS THE DIFFERENCE BETWEEN MEN'S WANTS AND WOMEN'S NEEDS? 73
- HOW DO WE MEET EACH OTHER IN THE MIDDLE? 74
- HOW DO WE COMPROMISE AND COMPLIMENT? 76
- HOW DO WE FULFILL EACH OTHER'S GOALS, DREAMS, AND VISIONS? 77
- HOW DO WE ADDRESS ISSUES AND CHALLENGES IN A RELATIONSHIP? 79

CONFLICT RESOLUTIONS 82

- CHALLENGING RELATIONSHIP QUESTIONS 83
  - HOW DO YOU ADDRESS THE PEBBLE IN YOUR SHOE? 85
  - ADDRESSING THE ELEPHANT IN THE ROOM 87
  - ADDRESSING ICING (BEING COLD, WALKING AWAY, NOT ADDRESSING THE ISSUES, ETC.) 89
  - ADDRESSING THE EGGSHELL ENVIRONMENT 91
  - ADDRESSING GASLIGHTING 93
  - HOW DO WE COLLABORATE? 94
  - HOW DO YOU DANCE DURING A STORM? 96
  - CONFLICT RESOLUTION TIPS 97
- ADDRESSING ISSUES 98
  - ADDRESSING PAST HURT (PRE-RELATIONSHIP) 100
  - ADDRESSING DIVORCE AND SEPARATION 101
  - ADDRESSING ADDICTION ISSUES 102
  - ADDRESSING PORN ADDICTIONS 104
  - ADDRESSING CO-PARENTING 105
  - ADDRESSING THE CHORE LIST 106
  - TOOLS TO HELP ADDRESS THE PAST 107
- PARENTING EACH OTHER 110
  - PARENTING IN A RELATIONSHIP 111
  - AVOID PARENTING IN THE RELATIONSHIP 112
  - CONTROLLING IN A RELATIONSHIP 114
  - AVOID CONTROLLING IN THE RELATIONSHIP 115
  - STOP PUTTING EACH OTHER DOWN 116
  - ADDRESSING ISSUES AND PROBLEMS 118
  - SEPARATE ISSUES FROM EACH OTHER 119
  - AGREE TO DISAGREE 121
- PRACTICAL FERTILIZERS 124
  - CULTIVATE RELATIONSHIP 125

GROW LOVE 127
BE AFFECTIONATE.. 128
NECESSARY AND MANDATORY...................................... 130
AFFECTION AND SEX... 131
SEX AND INTIMACY 133
EFFECTIVE COMMUNICATION 135
RIDE CONVERSATIONS AS A SPEAKER AND LISTENER .. 137
BUILDING TRUST... 138
LOVE LANGUAGES.. 139
RELATIONSHIP FERTILIZERS.. 141
BATHE RELATIONSHIPS WITH POSITIVE FERTILIZERS... 142
TOOLS TO HELP FERTILIZE THE RELATIONSHIP 143

KISSING BREAKUPS GOODBYE 144
DIGNITY AND RESPECT.. 146
FALLING IN LOVE, DATING AND HAVING FUN 147
"FIRST LOVE SYNDROME"... 148
BEST, BETTER, BONUS 149
OUR PHYSICAL AND MENTAL HEALTH........................ 151
GROOMING 152
CULTURE... 153
INTIMACY WITH CHILDREN IN THE HOME 155
TOOLS TO KISSING BREAKUPS GOODBYE................ 156

THE FOUR QUADRANTS 158
FRIENDSHIP 160
RELATIONSHIP 161
PARTNERSHIP... 162
COMPANIONSHIP 164

- TOOLS TO HAVE A HEALTHY, LONG-LASTING RELATIONSHIP 165
- BUILDING CONFIDENCE 167
  - PULL OUT THE BEST 169
  - DOMINATE A RELATIONSHIP WITH LOVE 170
  - MAXIMIZE LOVE IN A RELATIONSHIP 171
  - APPRECIATION 173
  - START A GRATITUDE JAR 174
  - BE AN ASSET 175
  - AVOID POINTING FINGERS 176
  - COMPROMISE 177
  - SERVING 179
  - LOVE INFINITELY 180
  - TOOLS TO BUILD CONFIDENCE 181
- CONCLUSION 183

INTRODUCTION

In the quest for a fulfilling, healthy, and enduring relationship, individuals often find themselves navigating a labyrinth of emotional complexities, communication barriers, and conflicting needs and desires. Cultivating a meaningful relationship while balancing individual growth can be both deeply rewarding and undeniably challenging. Relationships aren't solely about finding the right person—they're about becoming the right person. This journey involves continuous self-discovery, adaptation, and aligning values and goals with your partner.

To thrive, having a comprehensive and multi-faceted guide is invaluable. Imagine a resource crafted not just to explore the emotional and romantic aspects of relationships but also to illuminate the often-overlooked dimensions of friendship, partnership, and personal growth. Such a holistic approach ensures that you're not just falling in love but continually growing in love, allowing your connection to deepen and evolve.

What sets this guide apart is its balanced focus on individual reflection and mutual discovery. Healthy relationships are rooted in self-awareness. Before you can truly understand what you need from a partner, it's vital to uncover your own emotional needs, values, and desires. Reflective exercises inspire meaningful inner dialogue, while shared activities encourage open communication and foster emotional intimacy. This dual approach ensures that while your relationship grows stronger, you are also growing as an individual, creating a balance that enriches both your partnership and personal journey.

Love is often discussed in poetic terms, but real-world relationships require practical tools. This guide bridges the gap between ideals and actionable advice. Whether it's improving communication, resolving conflicts constructively, or deepening intimacy, the exercises provided can make an immediate difference in your relationship's quality. With an incremental approach, you'll have time to absorb and practice new insights, allowing growth to unfold naturally and sustainably.

This book is not limited to a specific life stage. Whether you're in the early stages of dating, years into marriage, or single and preparing for future relationships, the tools and activities are adaptable. This versatility means you can revisit the resource at different points in your life, discovering new perspectives as your needs and circumstances evolve.

Grounded in psychological theories, empirical research, and best practices from relationship counseling, the guide offers evidence-based strategies for navigating life's complexities together. This foundation enhances its credibility, ensuring the insights and tools provided are effective and transformative.

Relationships are dynamic, not static. They evolve as individuals grow and as life presents new challenges. This guide fosters a mindset of lifelong learning, encouraging you to refine your relationship skills continually and adapt to new phases and hurdles. It becomes a resource you can return to time and again—a trusted companion that grows with you.

To help you measure your progress, the guide includes regular assessments. These introspective exercises allow you to evaluate your growth, identify areas for improvement, and celebrate milestones in your relationship journey. This process not only fosters intentionality but also helps you track the depth of your connection and the strides you've made together.

T he ultimate reward of engaging with this guide is empowerment. With tools, insights, and a deeper understanding of both yourself and your partner, you'll be better equipped to navigate the complexities of relationships with confidence and grace. This empowerment doesn't just enhance your romantic connection; it enriches your overall emotional well-being, contributing to a more joyful and fulfilled life.

What Will You Gain?

1. **A Deeper Understanding of Yourself and Your Relationship Needs:** Relationships often falter not from a lack of love but from a lack of understanding. This guide helps you uncover your core values, emotional triggers, and deeply ingrained patterns, laying the foundation for meaningful and harmonious connections. Self-awareness is the first step toward building a thriving relationship.
2. **Mastery of Communication and Conflict Resolution Skills:** Miscommunication is a common relational pitfall, but effective communication can transform relationships. With this guide, you'll learn how to actively listen, express yourself constructively, and handle disagreements with empathy. These skills transform conflicts into opportunities for mutual understanding and growth.
3. **Insights into Emotional and Physical Intimacy:** Intimacy extends far beyond the physical. This guide delves into the intricate dynamics of emotional closeness, exploring love languages, prioritizing quality time, and fostering deeper

connections. You'll cultivate a bond that is both profound and enduring, enriching your partnership in every way.

4. **Practical Tools for Sustaining Long-term Relationship Health:** Lasting love requires effort, adaptability, and intention. From reigniting passion to navigating co-parenting or shared finances, you'll gain tools to nurture your relationship's core while addressing life's inevitable challenges.
5. **Creating a Culture of Respect, Love, and Appreciation:** Strong relationships are rooted in mutual respect and love. This guide empowers you to set healthy boundaries, appreciate your partner's contributions, and honor individuality. Building a culture of trust and connection ensures that both partners feel valued and secure.
6. **A Commitment to Lifelong Growth and Adaptation:** Relationships, like people, are constantly evolving. This guide emphasizes lifelong learning, helping you to adapt as your bond and circumstances change. Embracing growth together keeps your relationship dynamic and full of potential.

At its heart, this journey is about transformation—not just of your relationship but of yourself. It's about stepping into a fuller understanding of what relationships can be: spaces for joy, trust, connection, and shared purpose. Relationships thrive when both individuals are committed to growth, discovery, and intentional love.

Through self-awareness, actionable tools, and a mindset of lifelong learning, you can create a relationship that doesn't just survive but thrives. You'll build a connection that reflects mutual respect, shared dreams, and unshakable love—a bond that enriches every aspect of life.

NOTE:

*Please note partner refers to Spouse, Common-law, and Co-habitants

PURPOSE AND VALUE

In the realm of human experiences, relationships hold a special place. They are the intricate webs that connect us to the world and, more importantly, to each other. Through relationships, we navigate the complexities of life—its joys, sorrows, triumphs, and challenges. But as with any intricate web, the threads that bind us can become tangled or frayed if not carefully maintained. This chapter aims to explore the foundational aspects of relationships by focusing on their purpose and value. Before striving for healthier, more fulfilling connections with others, we must understand what drives us to seek these bonds and what we hope to achieve through them.

Understanding the essence of relationships requires us to consider multiple facets of human interaction. We need to ponder not just the emotional highs but also the compromises, the sacrifices, and even the mundane day-to-day interactions that create the fabric of a lasting bond. Relationships are not static entities; they are dynamic and ever-changing. They can be as fragile as they are resilient, as challenging as they are rewarding. Therefore, a nuanced understanding of what makes a relationship tick is essential for sustenance.

This chapter sets the stage for a deeper exploration into the dynamics of various types of relationships—romantic, platonic, or

PURPOSE AND VALUE

familial. We begin by examining the fundamental purpose of relationships. Why do we seek them out? What void do they fill, or what aspirations do they help us achieve? Understanding the purpose is the first step in appreciating the complexities involved in human connections.

Next, we dive into the motivations behind our desire to be in relationships. The human psyche is a complex structure of needs, desires, and fears. By examining the psychological factors that propel us toward relationships, we can better appreciate why they are a critical part of the human experience. This understanding also allows us to differentiate between healthy motivations and those rooted in emotional or psychological gaps a relationship cannot fill.

Another crucial area we focus on is giving and taking in a relationship. It's easy to dwell on what we gain from relationships, but it's equally important if not more so, to understand what we bring to the table. A balanced relationship is not a zero-sum game where one party's gain is another's loss; it's more of a mutual investment that pays dividends in emotional support, personal growth, and shared experiences.

We will also explore the practical aspects of maintaining a relationship. From the obstacles that can derail a relationship to the importance of setting realistic expectations, this chapter provides a comprehensive view of the challenges and rewards that come with being in a relationship. Lastly, we'll discuss tools and strategies that can help establish and sustain your relationships' purpose and value.

By the end of this chapter, the aim is to equip you with a well-rounded understanding of the fundamental aspects of relationships. With this foundation, you will be better prepared to engage in meaningful connections that are fulfilling and sustainable in the long run.

Addressing Needs, Wants, & Desires
What is the Purpose of a Relationship?

When we talk about relationships, we are essentially talking about multifaceted human interactions that manifest in various forms, such as romantic involvements, friendships, and family bonds. The underlying reason for the existence of these relationships is to establish a connection between two or more individuals. This connection is not just superficial or physical; it goes deep into emotional, psychological, and sometimes even spiritual realms.

The concept of interdependence in relationships is crucial. It suggests that the parties involved rely on each other differently, creating a balanced dynamic. For example, in a parent-child relationship, the child depends on the parent for guidance and sustenance. In contrast, the parent derives emotional fulfillment and a sense of purpose from caring for the child.

One of the most evident roles a relationship plays is in providing emotional support. When you are part of a healthy relationship, you have someone to turn to during your times of need. Whether you had a difficult day at work or are going through a significant life change, having someone who can offer emotional stability is invaluable.

Additionally, relationships serve as a channel for social validation. Society often judges individuals based on their social connections, and being in a relationship can sometimes offer a 'stamp of approval,' so to speak, that you are a person worthy of someone else's time and affection. But beyond societal perspectives, this social validation can also bring about a sense of personal accomplishment and happiness.

Shared experiences are another cornerstone of relationships. These are the collective memories and events that shape the relationship's narrative. Whether it's a romantic vacation, the birth of a child, or a simple movie night, these shared experiences contribute to a deeper understanding and bonding between individuals involved in the relationship.

Moreover, relationships offer a conducive environment for personal growth. A supportive partner or friend can provide constructive criticism that may be difficult to accept from others. This feedback mechanism is invaluable for self-improvement.

Finally, a sense of belonging and love is at the heart of any relationship. These primal emotions are deeply embedded in human psychology and provide the adhesive that holds relationships together over the long term.

Why Do We Desire or Want to Be in a Relationship?

The desire to be in a relationship is a fundamental human urge rooted in our evolutionary history. As social animals, human survival once depended on community involvement. While we have advanced far beyond the early communal living arrangements, the core need for social interaction remains.

Isolation or a lack of meaningful human contact can result in a range of adverse emotional and psychological outcomes, including depression and anxiety. Relationships act as a buffer against these negative effects by providing emotional stability. When you know someone has your back, it creates a sense of security that is psychologically reassuring.

Moreover, relationships enrich our lives by adding a layer of depth to our experiences. Whether it's the joy of achieving a mutual goal or the comfort derived from sharing a hardship, these shared experiences are magnified when lived through a relationship. It's like having a mirror that reflects your image and amplifies your emotional landscape.

What We Can Give and Not What We Can Get

The sustainability of a relationship often hinges on its underlying dynamic. If a relationship is solely fueled by what one party can extract from it—financial benefits, social standing, or even emotional support—such an arrangement will likely deteriorate over time. This is because an exploitative dynamic usually leads to resentment and emotional detachment.

Conversely, focusing on what you can contribute to the relationship creates a sense of balance. This can be as straightforward as providing emotional support when your partner is going through a difficult time or as complex as making career sacrifices to better align with your collective long-term goals.

When both individuals are invested in each other's well-being, it fosters an environment where the relationship is more likely to thrive. This mutual investment creates a nurturing atmosphere built on the foundation of reciprocal love and respect.

Additionally, the act of giving or contributing to a relationship can be rewarding in itself. It can lead to a more enduring sense of fulfillment and happiness than the fleeting joy derived from receiving. By setting the stage for a balanced, reciprocal relationship, you lay down the building blocks for a lasting connection.

What Are We Willing to Give Up and Compromise?

The dynamics of a relationship frequently necessitate adjustments and accommodations from both parties involved. These alterations could range from minor tweaks in daily habits to significant life-changing decisions. To begin with, time and personal space often become limited resources when you enter a relationship. Your hours are no longer solely your own; they are shared with another person with their needs, wants, and expectations. This often means sacrificing some of your leisure time or reorganizing your schedule to accommodate the relationship's needs.

Furthermore, career decisions can also be heavily influenced by a relationship. For example, an excellent job opportunity in another city might conflict with your partner's career or educational pursuits. In such

PURPOSE AND VALUE

cases, a serious discussion and potentially a compromise are required to align both parties' goals and aspirations.

The crux of the willingness to make these sacrifices often comes down to how much you value the relationship. Substantial sacrifices can seem justified if the relationship is seen as a cornerstone of your life. However, this willingness should be tempered by a balanced evaluation of what you are giving up and gaining. Notably, both individuals should feel they are contributing to the relationship to maintain a sense of equity and prevent resentment or exploitation.

It's also vital to consider the long-term implications of the compromises being made. Some sacrifices might be acceptable in the short term but could lead to regret or conflict if they compromise core aspects of your identity or life goals over the long term.

Some Obstacles That Can Become Problems in a Relationship?

A multitude of potential hurdles can arise in the course of a relationship, and the list is far from exhaustive. One of the most common problems is a lack of effective communication. Whether it's not discussing feelings openly, keeping secrets, or simply failing to articulate needs and expectations clearly, poor communication can severely hamper the health of a relationship.

Trust issues are another significant concern. These can arise from various circumstances—past betrayals, insecurities, or even external factors like social pressures. Once trust is eroded, rebuilding is challenging and can cast a long shadow over the relationship.

Financial difficulties often bring added stress and can strain a relationship. Money-related issues can stem from differing spending habits, income disparities, or unexpected financial setbacks like job loss or medical emergencies.

Addressing Needs, Wants, & Desires

Additionally, divergent life goals can pose a severe challenge. If one partner aspires to a high-powered career and the other desires a simple, family-oriented life, reconciling these aspirations can be problematic.

External pressures, such as work stress or family issues, can also indirectly affect a relationship. These external factors can exacerbate or create new problems, especially if they are not adequately managed or discussed.

The key to overcoming these obstacles lies in identifying them early and addressing them proactively. Ignoring these issues or downplaying their significance often results in a slow relationship degradation, culminating in its eventual breakdown.

What Are Expectations Brought into Relationships?

Every relationship comes with implicit or explicit expectations that serve as its foundational structure. These expectations can cover a broad spectrum of elements, from emotional and psychological to practical and material. Emotional support, for instance, is a common expectation: the idea that your partner will be there for you in times of emotional distress. Loyalty and fidelity are often considered non-negotiables in a committed relationship.

On a more practical level, some people expect their partners to contribute to household chores or share financial responsibilities. These tangible aspects are often easier to measure but are no less significant than emotional or psychological expectations.

However, problems often arise when these expectations are either unrealistic or not communicated clearly. For example, expecting your partner to always know what you're feeling without verbal communication is unrealistic and unfair. Similarly, if one partner expects a luxurious lifestyle that the other cannot provide, this mismatch can lead to conflict.

To prevent such issues, it's imperative to have open and honest conversations about what each individual expects from the relationship. These discussions can help align expectations and foster a relationship built on mutual understanding and respect. It's also beneficial to revisit these expectations periodically, as they can change over time due to various life events or personal growth.

What Gives Value to Relationships?

The notion of "value" in relationships is a complex construct encompassing various facets, each contributing to the overall sense of worth and meaningfulness that a relationship holds for the individuals involved. A foundational element in this construct is mutual respect. This is the idea that each partner acknowledges the other's individuality, choices, and freedom, valuing them not as an extension of themselves but as a separate entity with their own needs, desires, and aspirations.

Trust is another indispensable element that adds value to a relationship. Trust is not merely the absence of deceit or betrayal; it's the optimistic belief that the other person will act in your best interest, even when you are not around to witness it. This faith in each other's integrity forms the bedrock of a robust and valuable relationship.

Love, too, is a vital contributor to a relationship's value, but it's essential to recognize that love is a multi-dimensional emotion. It encompasses not just romantic love but also platonic love, familial love, and even a broader, more universal love that acknowledges the inherent worth of another human being.

In addition to these core elements, other factors like shared interests and compatible life goals can significantly enhance the value of a relationship. When two people enjoy shared activities, it provides a fertile ground for creating shared memories, which in turn strengthens the bond between them. Compatible life goals indicate that the two individuals are walking parallel paths, making it easier to support each other in meaningful ways.

Addressing Needs, Wants, & Desires

Moreover, a balanced give-and-take dynamic can be extremely valuable. This doesn't necessarily mean a 50-50 split in every responsibility or aspect but rather an overall sense of equality where both individuals feel they receive a fair degree of emotional and practical benefits in exchange for their contributions to the relationship.

The perception of value can differ from one individual to another, influenced by personal experiences, cultural background, and even current emotional state. Nonetheless, critical indicators like emotional well-being, opportunities for personal growth, and a sense of security and belonging often serve as universal markers for a valuable, meaningful relationship.

Why the Need to Recognize Value and Worth in a Relationship?

Recognizing the value and worth in a relationship serves multiple essential functions. First, it acts as an ongoing motivation for both parties to continue investing in the relationship. When you consciously acknowledge the value your relationship brings, it incentivizes you to devote time, energy, and emotional resources toward maintaining and even enhancing that value.

Second, recognizing your relationship's value helps establish and enforce healthy boundaries. When you are aware of what you bring to the relationship and what you gain from it, you are better equipped to define what is and isn't acceptable behaviour, both for yourself and your partner.

Third, this recognition fosters a sense of mutual benefit, which is essential for both individuals' long-term health and happiness. It helps to prevent a power imbalance or the feeling of being taken for granted, both of which can be detrimental to relationship longevity.

PURPOSE AND VALUE

Why Do We Need to Explore Our Self-Worth and Self-Value?

The exploration of self-worth and self-value is not merely an exercise in self-indulgence or introspection; it is a critical aspect of creating and maintaining healthy relationships. When you clearly understand your self-worth, you are less likely to settle for relationships that don't meet your needs or align with your values. Conversely, if you underestimate your self-worth, you may end up in relationships where you give more than you receive, leading to emotional exhaustion and a skewed power dynamic.

Knowing your worth and value allows you to enter relationships from a position of strength and confidence rather than desperation or dependence. It enables you to negotiate your needs and wants more effectively, thereby setting the stage for a relationship built on mutual respect and balanced give-and-take.

Moreover, understanding your self-value provides a touchstone for evaluating the health of your relationship. If you find yourself in a relationship that consistently undermines your self-worth, that's a clear indicator that something needs to change. Conversely, a relationship that enhances your sense of self-value is likely worth investing in.

Understanding self-worth and self-value is foundational to establishing, maintaining, and evaluating all forms of relationships. It serves as both a protective mechanism and a guiding light, helping you navigate the complex emotional landscape of human interaction.

How Do You Identify Worth and Value in a Relationship?

Determining the worth and value of a relationship is an intricate task involving objective and subjective measures. Mutual respect serves as a foundational criterion. It manifests in how each partner treats the other, not just in grand gestures but also in everyday interactions.

Respectful behaviour includes active listening, acknowledging the other person's viewpoint even when disagreeing, and honouring personal boundaries.

Quality of communication is another key indicator. Effective communication goes beyond merely exchanging information; it involves emotional openness, honesty, and the ability to share vulnerabilities without fear of judgment. The frequency, depth, and quality of conversations can often serve as a barometer for the overall health and value of the relationship.

Emotional support offers another benchmark. In a high-worth relationship, both partners feel emotionally safe and secure. They know they have a dependable ally in each other, someone who will stand by them through the ups and downs of life. This form of emotional backing often provides a sense of well-being, another intangible yet invaluable asset in a relationship.

Time and emotional investment are more quantifiable measures. Time spent together—particularly quality time that enriches the relationship—can indicate how much each person values the other. Emotional investment is trickier to measure but can be observed in the willingness to make sacrifices, exhibit patience, and show unconditional love and support.

How Do We Bring Out the Value and Worth in a Relationship?

Enhancing the worth and value of a relationship requires proactive and continuous effort from all parties involved. Open, honest, and frequent communication is the cornerstone. Without effective dialogue, misunderstandings can occur, leading to unnecessary conflicts and emotional distance. Thus, discussing feelings, expectations, and concerns becomes crucial for relationship maintenance.

Dedicating quality time is another essential element. Time is a finite resource, and choosing to spend it with someone strongly indicates the relationship's value. Whether going on dates, cooking together, or simply engaging in meaningful conversations, these shared activities deepen emotional bonds and enrich the relationship.

Emotional support is vital, especially during trying times. Being emotionally available for your partner provides a safety net and strengthens the relationship's foundation. Support should be a two-way street, with both parties willing and able to provide emotional solace when needed.

Mutual respect keeps the relationship balanced and fulfilling. This involves acknowledging each other's individuality, validating feelings, and treating each other with dignity.

Regular reassessment and recalibration ensure the relationship remains equitable and aligned with both parties' evolving needs and circumstances. This could mean renegotiating household chores, discussing future plans, or even seeking professional help to navigate complicated emotional terrains.

Why Do We Need to Appreciate Skills, Knowledge, and Experience?

The appreciation of skills, knowledge, and experience in a relationship is vital for several reasons, each contributing to the relationship's overall health and sustainability. At a fundamental level, acknowledging and valuing these attributes affirms each person's individuality. It provides a form of validation beyond physical attraction or emotional compatibility, touching on who the person is at their core—what they know, what they can do, and what they've been through.

In the context of a relationship, this validation can be incredibly empowering. It can boost self-esteem and contribute to a more positive self-image, which, in turn, benefits the relationship by fostering a sense of security and self-assurance in each partner. When individuals feel secure in their worth, they are generally better equipped to contribute positively to a relationship through emotional support, problem-solving, or other forms of partnership.

Moreover, recognizing and appreciating each other's skills and talents introduce an additional layer of depth and complexity to the relationship. It can lead to a richer, more textured understanding of each other, making the relationship more interesting and fulfilling. For example, if one partner is an excellent cook and the other is knowledgeable about literature, each can introduce the other to new experiences and ways of thinking. These shared experiences not only provide opportunities for enjoyment but also for education and personal growth, adding another dimension to how each partner benefits from the relationship.

This leads to another significant point: the role of mutual appreciation as a catalyst for growth. In a supportive and appreciative environment, individuals are often more motivated to develop their skills and acquire new knowledge. This dynamic can lead to a virtuous cycle where each partner's growth and development further enhance the relationship's overall quality and depth, making it more resilient and adaptable to challenges.

Appreciating skills, knowledge, and experience can help during conflict or stress. Understanding each other's strengths can provide practical benefits in problem-solving or decision-making. For instance, if one partner is particularly good at financial planning while the other is skilled in interpersonal communication, these strengths can be leveraged to navigate challenges more effectively.

The appreciation of skills, knowledge, and experience goes beyond mere acknowledgment. It serves as a multifaceted tool that validates each individual, enriches the relationship's emotional and intellectual landscape, fosters a conducive environment for personal growth, and can even provide practical advantages in dealing with life's complexities. Therefore, it is an essential aspect of building and maintaining a healthy, satisfying relationship.

PURPOSE AND VALUE

Tools to Build Purpose and Value

1. **Open Communication**: Actively engage in dialogues about feelings, future plans, and immediate concerns. Make it a habit to check in with each other regularly.
2. **Quality Time**: Prioritize spending time together. Make room in your schedules for activities you enjoy or intimate conversations that deepen your connection.
3. **Emotional Support**: Be emotionally present and available, particularly when your partner is going through stressful or challenging times. Emotional availability enhances the bond and provides a sense of security.
4. **Boundaries**: Clearly define and respect each other's personal and emotional boundaries. This creates a safe space where both individuals can thrive.
5. **Mutual Interests**: Engage in shared activities or hobbies. This can be as simple as watching a favourite TV series together or as involved as taking up a sport or hobby.
6. **Professional Help**: Relationship counselling or therapy can provide valuable insights and coping strategies, particularly for persistent issues or conflicts that are hard to resolve.
7. **Self-Assessment Tools**: Utilize quizzes, questionnaires, or even professional assessments to evaluate the health and direction of the relationship periodically.
8. **Conflict Resolution Strategies**: Educate yourselves on effective methods to resolve conflicts. This can prevent disagreements from escalating and harming the relationship.
9. **Financial Planning**: Openly discuss financial responsibilities and future goals. Financial strain is a typical relationship stressor, and proactive planning can mitigate its impact.

By actively addressing these various aspects, you are better positioned to build and maintain a relationship that is rich in value and significance. The effort put into nurturing these elements will make the relationship fulfilling and contribute to personal growth and happiness for all individuals involved.

INVESTMENT

As we transition from understanding the foundational aspects of purpose and value in relationships, it's crucial to turn our focus toward the concept of investment. If the first week was about laying down the cornerstone of why relationships matter, this week serves as the blueprint for nurturing and sustaining them actively. Think of your relationship as a garden. While understanding purpose and value is akin to knowing the type of soil you have, the amount of sunlight your garden will get, and what plants are best suited for your environment, the concept of investment is the actual act of planting, watering, and tending to your garden. Without this critical step, even the most fertile soil remains barren.

Investment in a relationship is multi-dimensional; it's not just about time or money but also emotional energy, mental space, and even the sacrifices we make. Like in any successful enterprise, there's a notion of risk and reward. By putting in the effort, we hope to cultivate a relationship that is not only stable but also enriching and fulfilling. Yet, there's also the understanding that there are no guarantees. Investments can yield high returns, but they can also fail. However, without taking the risk of investing in the first place, the prospect of any returns—emotional, psychological, or even physical—is virtually null.

INVESTMENT

At the heart of this chapter is the idea that relationships are not just static constructs but dynamic entities that require ongoing care and attention. This is akin to running a business, where market conditions change, consumer preferences evolve, and the organization itself goes through various life cycles. To keep a business thriving, continuous investment in the form of capital, innovation, and human resources is essential. Similarly, ongoing contributions of love, time, emotional support, and other vital "relationship resources" are necessary to keep a relationship vibrant and healthy.

The subsequent sections will delve into what it means to invest in a relationship, drawing parallels with the world of business to provide a unique lens through which to examine this concept. We will explore the idea of couples as business partners in the venture, that is, their relationship—each bringing their strengths, weaknesses, assets, and liabilities to the table. We'll discuss the nuances of communication, a cornerstone of successful businesses and relationships, and how to avoid the pitfalls of misunderstandings or ambiguous intimations.

Furthermore, we'll tackle the critical issue of personal and relational growth. Just like a successful business needs to adapt, innovate, and expand to stay competitive, a fulfilling relationship requires growth and adaptation to keep both partners engaged and satisfied. This chapter will provide you with the tools needed to identify areas for growth and the strategies to achieve it.

As we move through this week's topic of investment, think of each section as a guide to a different aspect of this complex but rewarding endeavour. Just as a financial advisor would guide you through the intricacies of investment portfolios, consider this chapter your relationship investment advisor, providing you with the insights and tools you need to make informed, influential contributions to your most valuable asset—your relationship.

Addressing Needs, Wants, & Desires
What Does It Mean to Invest in a Relationship?

Investing in a relationship is a multifaceted endeavour transcending the simplistic notion of merely allocating time or other resources to someone else. At its core, investing in a relationship implies a deliberate and sustained effort to enrich, strengthen, and grow the mutual bond between you and your partner. It's about making conscious choices that contributing to the relationship's well-being, longevity, and overall quality. This investment can manifest in various forms—emotional, cognitive, and tangible—each contributing uniquely to the fabric of the relationship.

When we talk about emotional investment, we're referring to the provision of emotional support, love, and companionship. This entails being there for your partner during challenging times, celebrating their accomplishments, and sharing the intimate details of your life. Emotional investment fosters a feeling of safety and trust, acting as the glue that holds the relationship together. It involves actively caring for your partner's emotional well-being, acknowledging their feelings, and providing a compassionate and understanding ear when needed. This kind of emotional backing often creates a sense of psychological well-being, a priceless component of a meaningful relationship.

Cognitive investment involves intellectual engagement with the relationship's dynamics, future, and potential challenges. It means thinking critically about the relationship, from contemplating shared goals and aspirations to planning for practicalities like living arrangements or financial planning. Cognitive investment also includes actively resolving conflicts through thoughtful discussion and compromise. This cognitive aspect is where strategies are formed, from deciding how to balance career and family life to planning vacations or future life milestones. It's akin to the planning and strategizing a business owner might do to ensure long-term success.

On the tangible side, investment may include financial contributions or specific actions that facilitate the relationship's daily functioning or long-term goals. This could range from taking on

INVESTMENT

household responsibilities and chores to making career sacrifices to be closer to each other. Financial investment can also come into play, whether pooling resources to buy a home, planning for retirement, or simply managing daily expenses. These tangible investments have a genuine impact on the quality and stability of the relationship, forming the structural framework upon which emotional and cognitive investments can flourish.

Investing in a relationship also inherently involves a degree of commitment. This commitment isn't just about exclusivity or longevity but about a dedicated focus on mutual growth and happiness. It means choosing to prioritize the relationship, even when it's challenging or inconvenient. It's about making sacrifices and compromises that may not offer immediate gratification but contribute to the relationship's long-term health and happiness.

Investment often comes with sacrifices. These sacrifices can be as simple as compromising on a restaurant choice or as significant as moving to a new city for your partner's job opportunity. These are active choices made to nurture and sustain the relationship. However, the willingness to make these sacrifices should be rooted in a balanced understanding of the relationship's overall give-and-take, ensuring that both partners feel their contributions are acknowledged and valued.

Investing in a relationship is a complex, ongoing process that involves a balanced blend of emotional, cognitive, and tangible contributions. It's about creating a nurturing environment where both partners can thrive, setting the stage for a relationship that is not just enduring but also enriching and fulfilling for everyone involved.

Why Should a Relationship Be Considered a Business?

The idea of treating a relationship like a business may initially seem counterintuitive or even unromantic. However, the analogy holds substantial merit when dissected further. In a business partnership, individuals come together to combine their skills, resources, and time to

Addressing Needs, Wants, & Desires

achieve a common objective—usually to generate profit and create value. Similarly, in a romantic relationship, two individuals unite to share their lives, aiming for mutual happiness, emotional fulfillment, and, in many cases, the building of a family.

When managing a business, partners are required to strategize, set goals, and evaluate outcomes. This involves financial planning, resource allocation, risk assessment, and contingency planning. Likewise, in a relationship, couples need to engage in emotional and practical planning. This could involve anything from deciding the dynamics of household chores and financial responsibilities to discussing future plans, such as whether to have children, where to live and career aspirations.

In a business, regular audits and performance reviews are essential for identifying areas for improvement and growth. Similarly, periodic evaluation of a relationship is crucial for its long-term health. This could involve open dialogues about satisfaction levels, emotional needs, and future expectations.

Moreover, just like in business, transparency and clear communication are crucial in a relationship. A business cannot thrive if the partners are unclear about their expectations, responsibilities, and contributions. Similarly, a relationship can only flourish when both parties are transparent about their feelings, expectations, and concerns.

While the currencies of exchange may differ—emotional satisfaction and love instead of money—the fundamental principles of partnership, investment, planning, communication, and mutual growth remain constant in both business partnerships and romantic relationships.

Are Couples Considered Partners in the Business of a Relationship?

When we apply the business analogy to relationships, couples indeed become akin to business partners, jointly managing the enterprise that is their shared life. Each partner brings unique "assets"

INVESTMENT

into this enterprise, ranging from emotional support and love to financial stability or specific skills and expertise.

Just like business partners have defined roles based on their skills and contributions to the enterprise, couples also often naturally fall into roles within the relationship. For example, one partner may be better at handling finances, while the other excels at emotional caregiving. These roles are not static and can evolve over time as the relationship matures and individual circumstances change.

Furthermore, successful business partnerships are built on a foundation of mutual respect, trust, and shared objectives. These elements are equally, if not more, crucial in romantic relationships. Both parties must respect each other's individuality, trust one another implicitly, and align their long-term goals and values for the relationship to be successful.

It's also worth noting that successful businesses often benefit from the synergy created by their partners' complementary skills and efforts. In relationships, the concept of synergy is equally applicable. When two people bring different but complementary skills, perspectives, and emotional resources, the relationship often becomes more significant than the sum of its parts. This synergistic effect can lead to a more enriched, fulfilling, and resilient relationship.

In the business of relationships, the "profits" are not monetary but emotional and psychological: happiness, emotional security, personal growth, and the joy of shared experiences and mutual achievements. Just like a business requires ongoing effort, attention to detail, and the willingness to adapt and evolve, so does a successful, long-term romantic relationship.

How Do We Avoid Intimations?

The term "intimations" often refers to subtle hints, vague suggestions, or indirect messages that people might use to express their feelings or desires. While this form of communication may seem less

Addressing Needs, Wants, & Desires

confrontational, it can lead to misunderstandings, misinterpretations, and, ultimately, conflicts within a relationship. This is particularly problematic regarding essential matters like emotional needs, relationship expectations, or conflicts that require resolution.

Adopting a clear, straightforward communication style is essential to avoid intimation pitfalls. Instead of expecting your partner to interpret vague signals or read between the lines, it's crucial to explicitly articulate your thoughts, feelings and needs. The first step in achieving this is self-awareness. You need to understand what you truly want or feel before you can communicate it effectively to your partner.

Transparency is the next key ingredient. When you're transparent, you remove ambiguity from the equation. This minimizes the risk of misunderstandings and contributes to building trust. If you're concerned about how your message might be received, you can employ techniques such as "I-statements" to express yourself in a non-accusatory manner. For example, instead of saying, "You never listen to me," you can say, "I feel unheard when you don't pay attention to what I'm saying."

Regularly scheduled open dialogues can also be beneficial. These are opportunities to discuss the logistics of your shared life and forums to express any underlying concerns or unspoken expectations. This proactive approach can preemptively resolve issues that might otherwise have only become apparent through intimations or passive-aggressive behaviour.

How Do We Identify the Need to Grow the Relationship?

Every relationship goes through phases, and it's entirely natural for the intensity of initial attraction to evolve into a more stable, less exhilarating form of love. However, it's essential to distinguish between comfortable stability and detrimental stagnation. The latter can be a breeding ground for discontent, resentment, or even infidelity.

INVESTMENT

How do you recognize the signs that your relationship needs to grow? One indicator could be a feeling of emotional or romantic unfulfillment. If you find that your interactions with your partner have become perfunctory or routine, lacking in emotional depth or intimacy, it may be time to inject new life into the relationship.

Frequent conflicts over trivial matters can be another sign. While some conflict is natural and even healthy in a relationship, consistent bickering over inconsequential issues may point to deeper, unresolved problems. These conflicts often serve as a proxy for underlying dissatisfaction or emotional disconnect.

A waning of the initial passion and excitement is another standard indicator. While it's unrealistic to expect the honeymoon phase to last forever, a complete absence of romantic or sexual energy can signal a need for rejuvenation and growth within the relationship.

Regular "relationship check-ins" can serve as a structured way to assess the need for growth. During these conversations, you can discuss your feelings openly, evaluate the state of your relationship, and identify areas for improvement or investment.

If you notice any of these signs, it's not a cause for immediate alarm, but it is a signal that you might need to invest more time, effort, and emotional energy into your relationship. Growth can come in many forms—be it through spending more quality time together, improving your communication, setting new shared goals, or even seeking couples counselling to resolve more complex issues.

Tools to Keep Investing in the Relationship

1. **Regular Check-ins**: Schedule periodic conversations to discuss the relationship's health, address concerns, and plan for the future.
2. **Financial Planning**: Mutual goals like buying a house, planning vacations, or saving for retirement require financial planning.

Addressing Needs, Wants, & Desires

Being on the same page financially can significantly strengthen the relationship.

3. **Date Nights**: Never underestimate the power of quality time. Regular date nights can keep the romantic spark alive and provide an opportunity for a more profound emotional connection.
4. **Conflict Resolution Skills**: Learn and apply effective conflict resolution techniques to address disagreements constructively rather than allowing them to escalate.
5. **Counselling and Therapy**: Professional help is not just for relationships in crisis. Therapists can offer valuable insights and tools for relationship growth and maintenance.
6. **Personal Growth**: Sometimes, investing in your personal growth can be a powerful way to invest in your relationship. Whether gaining new skills, improving your emotional intelligence, or even physical fitness, personal improvements often translate into relationship improvements.
7. **Affection and Appreciation**: Simple acts of kindness and expressions of gratitude can go a long way in nurturing a relationship. These affirm your commitment and appreciation for your partner.
8. **Shared Activities**: Engaging in activities that both of you enjoy can deepen your connection and create lasting memories.
9. **Boundaries and Personal Space**: Paradoxically, allowing each other personal space to grow can also be an investment in the relationship. Respecting boundaries makes the time spent together more meaningful.

By approaching your relationship as a mutual investment, you pave the way for sustained growth and enrichment. It requires ongoing effort, keen attention to each other's needs, and the agility to adapt and evolve. Like a successful business venture, a fulfilling relationship is built on the principles of mutual benefit, shared objectives, and a lot of hard work and dedication.

UNDERSTANDING

In the intricate dance that is a long-term relationship, the steps you take are often influenced by your feelings for your partner and the depth of your understanding of each other. This understanding goes beyond knowing each other's favourite colour or preferred type of cuisine. It delves deep into the labyrinth of personal psychologies, emotional triggers, and medical conditions that could influence behaviour and mutual interactions. Achieving this comprehensive understanding is neither simple nor immediate; it's a continuous process that evolves as you spend more time together, facing life's challenges side-by-side.

This week's chapter focuses on the crucial elements contributing to a well-rounded understanding of yourself and your partner. We explore why it's beneficial to concentrate on each other's strengths rather than weaknesses, shedding light on the positive impact this focus can have on your mutual emotional well-being and the overall health of your relationship. We delve into the complexities of personality and character traits, examining how they influence individual behaviours and interaction styles within the partnership.

Addressing Needs, Wants, & Desires

Moreover, we tackle some more challenging aspects of relationships: insecurities, low self-esteem, and the myriad of mental health issues that can introduce additional complexities. Understanding these elements is not just about labelling or diagnosing problems; it's about gaining insights that can lead to effective coping strategies and meaningful communication. We scrutinize how specific challenges like adult ADHD, bad habits, addictions, and even personality disorders like narcissistic traits can influence relationship dynamics. This section aims to equip you with the knowledge needed to navigate these challenges successfully, whether that involves direct communication, professional help, or a combination of both.

Furthermore, we address the importance of accepting imperfections, flaws, and even past mistakes. Every individual comes with their own set of baggage—emotional, psychological, or sometimes even legal. Learning to deal with this baggage is vital, especially when planning to build a future together. This chapter provides guidance on how to acknowledge these issues, discuss them openly, and, when possible, find closure.

Finally, we discuss the essential nature of boundaries and limitations. These invisible lines serve as critical markers that safeguard individuality, promote personal growth, and contribute to maintaining a healthy relationship balance. As you navigate this chapter, you'll encounter various tools and strategies designed to enhance your understanding of yourself and your partner. These tools range from empathy exercises and self-improvement resources to the potential benefits of professional counselling.

In short, this chapter aims to serve as a comprehensive guide to achieving a nuanced understanding of yourself and your partner. It's designed to equip you with the tools, knowledge, and insights you need to build a relationship that's not just loving but also profoundly understanding and mutually respectful. With this foundation, you're better prepared to face whatever challenges life may throw your way,

UNDERSTANDING

fortified by the knowledge that you truly understand the person standing beside you.

Understanding Each Other's Strengths

Understanding each other's strengths is a practice that extends far beyond mere acknowledgment or superficial recognition; it is a deliberate shift in perspective that can fundamentally alter the dynamics of a relationship for the better. The concept is rooted in the philosophy of positive psychology, which advocates for focusing on strengths to facilitate individual and collective well-being. By directing attention towards what each person brings to the relationship rather than what they may lack, you cultivate a more optimistic, appreciative atmosphere.

In practical terms, recognizing each other's strengths allows for a more effective division of roles and responsibilities within the relationship. For example, if one partner excels in financial planning while the other is better at emotional nurturing, acknowledging these strengths helps allocate responsibilities accordingly. This leads to a more efficient and harmonious partnership, where each person gets to contribute in ways that make them feel competent and valued.

Furthermore, when you focus on strengths, you enable each other to operate from a zone of expertise, which leads to a greater sense of fulfillment. This positive reinforcement creates a virtuous cycle: feeling competent in certain aspects enhances self-esteem, making each partner more willing and able to contribute to the relationship. Moreover, appreciating each other's strengths can lead to a deeper emotional connection, fostering mutual respect and admiration.

However, it's important to note that focusing on strengths does not mean ignoring weaknesses altogether. Instead, the idea is not to let those weaknesses dominate your view of the relationship or your partner. Constructive criticism and growth are essential, but they should come from a place of love and a desire to build up rather than tear down.

Addressing Needs, Wants, & Desires
Understanding Personality and Characters

Understanding each other's personalities and character traits is akin to acquiring a roadmap to navigate your relationship's intricate highways and byways. It is about grasping the fundamental aspects of your partner's nature—how they think, feel, and behave—and using that understanding to foster a deeper, more meaningful connection.

Personality traits, often categorized as Openness, Conscientiousness, Extraverts, Introverts, Agreeableness, and Neuroticism, offer insights into how each partner will likely respond to various situations. For example, an extroverted individual might derive energy from social interactions, while an introverted partner may find the same experiences draining. Knowing this can guide you in planning activities that both will enjoy or at least find a balanced compromise.

Moreover, understanding each other's character traits—such as integrity, compassion, or resilience—can provide valuable context when conflicts arise. For instance, if you know your partner values honesty above all else, you're less likely to misconstrue a blunt statement as rudeness.

Additionally, this understanding aids in setting realistic expectations for the relationship. If you know your partner is fiercely independent, expecting them to be constantly available for emotional support might lead to disappointment. On the flip side, knowing that your partner values emotional intimacy can help you make an effort to open up more, thereby meeting their needs while strengthening the relationship.

Identifying the strengths and advantages of characters and personalities is essential. Each one holds positive and negative attributes. Most of us focus on the negative attributes instead of the positives, and we try to convert each other to be like us. However, we need to appreciate the differences and utilize the positive attributes to bring gains to the relationship.

UNDERSTANDING

Addressing Insecurities, Lack of Confidence, and Low Self-Esteem

Insecurities, lack of confidence, and low self-esteem are emotional states that can significantly impact the dynamics of a relationship. They can manifest in various ways, such as excessive jealousy, constant need for validation, emotional volatility, and a tendency to misinterpret actions or words as personal attacks. These emotional vulnerabilities can create a cycle of negativity, affecting not only the person experiencing them but also their partner and the relationship. Addressing these issues is a multi-layered process, often involving individual self-improvement efforts and constructive engagement within the relationship.

The first step in addressing these emotional states is recognizing them within yourself. Self-awareness is crucial here, as it lays the foundation for self-improvement. Techniques like journaling, mindfulness exercises, and cognitive behavioural therapy (CBT) can be valuable tools for understanding your emotional triggers and patterns. Individual therapy can provide a safe space for exploring these vulnerabilities, offering coping mechanisms to build self-esteem and manage insecurities effectively.

Open dialogue about insecurities and low self-esteem is essential but can be challenging. The key is to express your feelings without blaming or accusing your partner. Using "I" statements can help focus the conversation on your experience, making it easier for your partner to understand your perspective without feeling attacked. For example, saying, "I feel insecure when you spend a lot of time with your friends and don't include me," is less confrontational than saying, "You make me feel insecure when you ignore me."

The partner's role in this context is to provide emotional support and constructive feedback. It's crucial to validate your partner's feelings without enabling their insecurities. This might mean offering reassurance but also setting healthy boundaries. For example, while it's reasonable to provide comfort, it's also essential to maintain your own personal space and friendships. The objective is to support your partner in their self-improvement journey without compromising your well-being.

For deeply-rooted insecurities and low self-esteem issues, professional help may be necessary. Couples therapy can offer a neutral ground for both partners to explore these issues. Therapists can provide expert guidance and tools for communication and emotional management that can be invaluable in resolving the underlying issues. Sometimes, individual therapy may also be recommended for the partner experiencing these emotional states, as it can offer a more focused environment for self-exploration and improvement.

Friends and family can also play a supportive role, offering an external perspective that can be valuable in understanding the dynamics of the relationship. However, maintaining boundaries is crucial to ensure the relationship's privacy is respected.

By proactively addressing insecurities, lack of confidence, and low self-esteem, you can build a healthier emotional foundation for your relationship. This involves a collaborative effort that respects both partners' emotional experiences while encouraging individual growth and self-improvement. It's a challenging but ultimately rewarding process that enhances the relationship's quality and contributes to personal development for both individuals involved.

Insecurities are deeply held fears or anxieties often stem from past experiences, societal expectations, or inherent vulnerabilities. They can be subtle and latent, emerging only under specific circumstances, or they can be pervasive, affecting many aspects of an individual's life. In the context of a romantic relationship, insecurities can manifest in various ways— from jealousy, possessiveness, and controlling behaviour to withdrawal, emotional unavailability, or even self-sabotage.

UNDERSTANDING

The impact of these insecurities is multifaceted. For one, they can erode the fundamental trust and safety vital for a healthy relationship. For instance, incessant jealousy can make the other partner feel constantly scrutinized and under suspicion, which is emotionally exhausting. On the flip side, the partner experiencing jealousy lives in constant anxiety and fear of abandonment.

Moreover, insecurities can create a destructive cycle. The insecure behaviour pushes the other person away, thereby confirming the insecure individual's fear of rejection or inadequacy, which fuels more insecurity. This self-perpetuating cycle can be incredibly damaging, leading to an emotional disconnect that might be irreparable if not addressed.

Being aware of both your own and your partner's insecurities is the first step toward mitigating their negative impacts. Once these insecurities are identified and openly discussed, you can work on strategies to assuage them. This often involves individual self-work and mutual efforts within the relationship, such as building trust through consistent and supportive behaviour.

Low self-confidence and self-esteem are issues that extend beyond the individual and profoundly impact the relational dynamic. Lack of self-confidence often manifests as an inability to assert oneself, make decisions, or express one's needs and desires. This creates an imbalance in the relationship, placing an undue burden on the other partner to fill these gaps. Over time, this imbalance can breed resentment on both sides—the more confident partner may feel burdened, while the less confident one may feel increasingly dependent and disempowered.

Low self-esteem can also result in emotional volatility. When someone doesn't value themselves highly, even minor conflicts or disagreements can trigger disproportionate emotional reactions. They might perceive criticisms or challenges as affirmations of their inadequacy, making it difficult to resolve issues or have honest discussions without causing emotional harm.

Low self-esteem can create an unhealthy dependency on the relationship for self-worth. This can be exhausting for the other partner and can lead to a toxic cycle where the person with low self-esteem becomes increasingly demanding of validation, pushing the other person further away.

Furthermore, low self-confidence and self-esteem can inhibit emotional intimacy. The fear of rejection or judgment may prevent the less confident partner from opening up, sharing vulnerabilities, or even engaging in constructive criticisms or conflicts. This limits the depth of emotional connection that can be achieved.

Addressing these issues is often a long-term process. It involves individual self-improvement efforts, such as therapy or self-help, and changes in the relational dynamic to create a more supportive and affirming environment. Open communication about these challenges and their underlying causes and potential solutions is essential for both partners to navigate this complex emotional landscape successfully.

Mistakes, Past Adverse History, Bad Habits, and Wrongdoing

One of the inevitable truths about human relationships is that no one is perfect. Every individual comes with a history, experiences, and actions that have shaped who they are today. Within this reality, mistakes and past adverse histories often loom large, particularly when they impact the dynamic between two individuals in a relationship.

Accepting past mistakes and adverse histories is not about dismissing their importance or ignoring the lessons they provide. It is about acknowledging that these events have occurred, discussing them openly to understand their implications, and then actively choosing to move beyond them. This process is critical for several reasons.

UNDERSTANDING

Firstly, it allows for genuine forgiveness, which is essential for emotional closure. Holding onto past mistakes often breeds resentment and distrust, which are corrosive elements in any relationship. Forgiveness doesn't necessarily mean forgetting; it means releasing the emotional hold of these past actions on the present relationship.

Secondly, this acceptance and closure pave the way for personal and relational growth. Once you've acknowledged and moved past these historical events, you can focus more clearly on the present and future of the relationship. This shift in focus can liberate and open new avenues for connection and mutual understanding.

Thirdly, it establishes a precedent for handling future conflicts or mistakes. No relationship is devoid of missteps or disagreements. Having a model for how to deal with them—accept, discuss, forgive, and move on—can be incredibly beneficial for the relationship's long-term health.

Accepting Imperfections, Flaws, and Weaknesses

The notion of accepting imperfections, flaws, and weaknesses in a relationship is deeply intertwined with the concept of unconditional love and emotional maturity. While it's common to enter relationships focusing on the attributes that attract us to our partners—physical appearance, intellectual compatibility, shared interests, or emotional chemistry—it's crucial to understand that no individual is devoid of flaws or imperfections.

By accepting imperfections, you're acknowledging the full spectrum of human complexity. This involves recognizing that your partner may have traits or habits you find less than ideal but choosing to love them anyway. Acceptance doesn't mean you ignore problematic behaviours or disregard how they affect you. Instead, it's about acknowledging these traits without judgment and deciding how to navigate them within the context of the relationship.

Why is this important? For one, acceptance creates a safe space where both individuals feel valued and loved for who they are, not an idealized version of themselves. This emotional safety is crucial for fostering intimacy and deep connection. Moreover, accepting your partner's flaws can make it easier for them to acknowledge and work on these issues, creating a constructive atmosphere for personal and relational growth.

Accepting imperfections also offers an opportunity for greater self-awareness. It forces you to confront your imperfections and consider whether you're also offering the same level of acceptance that you seek from your partner. This form of mutual acceptance forms the bedrock of a healthy, loving relationship.

Understanding Opinions and Perceptions

Opinions and perceptions are intricate mental constructs influenced by many factors such as upbringing, cultural background, education, and individual life experiences. These aspects of our cognitive framework play a critical role in how we interpret and interact with the world around us, including our relationships. Within a partnership, these opinions and perceptions can either harmonize to create a more fulfilling connection or clash, leading to misunderstandings and conflicts.

Recognizing that opinions and perceptions are inherently subjective is essential for fostering a healthy relationship. Every individual has a unique lens through which they view the world, shaped by countless experiences and influences over their lifetime. In a relationship, you essentially merge two distinct worldviews, each with its values, priorities, and interpretations. Understanding that these perspectives are not absolute truths but rather individualized interpretations can go a long way in fostering mutual respect and open dialogue.

For instance, disagreements in a relationship often stem not from factual inaccuracies but differing interpretations and priorities. Understanding this can guide conflict resolution strategies. Instead of attempting to prove the "correctness" of your viewpoint, the focus can shift to understanding the underlying perceptions and feelings that led to each partner's stance. This more empathetic and nuanced approach makes conflict resolution more straightforward and deepens the emotional connection between partners.

Understanding Mental Health, Including OCD and Perfectionism

Understanding the role of mental health in a relationship is a multifaceted endeavour that requires empathy, education, and often professional guidance. Let's take Obsessive-Compulsive Disorder (OCD) and perfectionism as specific examples. These are not mere quirks or preferences; they are conditions that significantly impact an individual's thought patterns, behaviours, and emotional well-being.

OCD is characterized by persistent, unwanted thoughts (obsessions) and repetitive behaviours or mental acts (compulsions) that the individual feels driven to perform. This can place a considerable emotional burden on both the individual and their partner. Understanding OCD means educating yourself about its symptoms, triggers, and treatment options. It also means avoiding the trivialization of these behaviours and instead approaching them with the gravity they deserve.

Perfectionism, while not always classified as a mental health disorder, can also significantly impact a relationship. A perfectionist's constant need for everything to meet impossibly high standards can lead to frustration, disappointment, and emotional withdrawal. If you're in a relationship with a perfectionist, understanding the motivations behind this behaviour can provide valuable insights into their emotional landscape.

Addressing Needs, Wants, & Desires

Both OCD and perfectionism can lead to emotional strain in a relationship, as they often result in increased anxiety, conflict, and misunderstanding. Therefore, understanding these conditions is not just a matter of compassion but also a practical necessity for maintaining a healthy relationship dynamic. Treatment often involves cognitive-behavioural therapy (CBT) or medication, and having a supportive partner can make a difference in treatment efficacy.

Understanding Organic-Related Issues

Navigating a relationship with someone affected with delirium, dementia, Alzheimer's disease, or amnesia can be challenging. The complexities go beyond the typical emotional and psychological dynamics of a partnership. These conditions are characterized by cognitive impairments that can significantly affect an individual's memory, problem-solving abilities, personality, and behaviour.

Understanding these conditions demands a multi-disciplinary approach involving medical advice, psychological insights, and often specialized caregiving skills. For instance, Alzheimer's disease can have a profound impact not only on the person suffering from it but also on their partner. Symptoms like memory loss, confusion, and disorientation can be emotionally distressing for both individuals. As the condition progresses, the caregiving partner may have to make increasingly difficult decisions regarding healthcare and living arrangements, often without the affected partner's complete comprehension or consent.

Delirium, usually acute and reversible, presents a different set of challenges. It can be triggered by medical conditions such as infections or medication, leading to fluctuating levels of consciousness and cognitive impairments. Understanding the root causes and potential treatments for delirium can help manage its immediate impact on the relationship and make informed healthcare decisions.

UNDERSTANDING

In cases of chronic conditions like dementia or Alzheimer's, long-term planning becomes crucial. This may involve tough decisions about potential institutional care versus home care, managing financial resources, and legal considerations such as power of attorney. For the partner, understanding these conditions is not just about healthcare but also emotional resilience, as they must reconcile with significant changes in their loved one's personality and capabilities.

Therefore, understanding these organic-related issues is about more than just knowledge; it's about emotional and practical preparation. It requires the unaffected partner to equip themselves with a range of coping mechanisms, from emotional support networks to professional healthcare guidance, to effectively manage this extremely challenging phase of their relationship.

Understanding Bad Habits, Addictions, and Behaviours

The presence of bad habits, addictions, or problematic behaviours in a relationship can be a significant point of tension and conflict. These issues often serve as persistent challenges that can derail the harmony and mutual respect within the relationship. Bad habits can range from minor annoyances like disorganization to disruptive behaviours like chronic lateness. On the other end of the spectrum, addictions to substances like alcohol drugs, or even behaviors like gambling can have devastating emotional, financial, and physical consequences.

Understanding these issues is the first step toward resolving them and requires a nuanced, compassionate approach. The goal is not merely to identify these habits or addictions but to delve into the underlying causes that drive them. Is it stress, a past trauma, or perhaps an undiagnosed psychological issue? Recognizing the root cause can help both partners find a constructive solution rather than merely treating the symptoms. For example, if a partner's drinking problem is linked to stress management, the solution may involve finding healthier coping mechanisms rather than merely insisting that they stop drinking.

Furthermore, some bad habits and addictions may require professional intervention, including medical treatment or therapy. Understanding the severity and scope of the issue can help you decide when it's time to seek external help. And it's essential to approach these issues as a team. Even if only one partner is exhibiting the bad habit or addiction, both are affected by it, and both have a role in finding a solution.

Understanding Personality Disorders and Narcissistic Traits

Navigating a relationship when one or both partners have a personality disorder or exhibit narcissistic traits adds layers of complexity and potential volatility to the dynamic. Personality disorders, such as narcissistic personality disorder, borderline personality disorder, or antisocial personality disorder, are characterized by enduring patterns of behaviour, cognition, and inner experience which deviate markedly from the expectations of the individual's culture. These disorders often result in emotional dysregulation and can significantly impact relationships.

Understanding these disorders is crucial but challenging, often requiring specialized knowledge and professional guidance. For example, narcissistic individuals may lack empathy and be excessively preoccupied with fantasies of unlimited success, power, or beauty. This could manifest as a lack of emotional support, manipulative behaviours, or a constant need for admiration in the relationship.

If a personality disorder is suspected, the first step is to seek a professional diagnosis and guidance on management strategies. Treatment for personality disorders often involves long-term psychotherapy and, sometimes, medication. It's essential for the partner without the disorder to educate themselves extensively on the condition and its implications, both for their well-being and to effectively support their partner.

Understanding these disorders also involves setting realistic expectations. While therapy can manage symptoms and improve quality of life, personality disorders are enduring and often involve deeply ingrained patterns of behaviour that are resistant to change. Therefore, it's essential to set boundaries to protect your emotional well-being while being realistic about the extent and speed of possible changes.

In short, understanding bad habits, addictions, and personality disorders requires a multi-faceted, often professional, approach. It involves identifying the issue, understanding its underlying causes or characteristics, and then employing a range of strategies for management and treatment. This long-term endeavour often requires patience, empathy, and sometimes professional help. The aim is to build a healthier, more balanced relationship that supports the well-being of both individuals.

Understanding Boundaries and Limitations

Understanding boundaries and limitations is a multifaceted aspect of relationship management that holds significant importance for the emotional well-being and mutual respect between partners. Boundaries can encompass a wide range of behaviours and expectations, from something as simple as personal space and alone time to more complex issues like emotional availability and financial responsibilities. They serve as invisible barriers that protect individuality, promote personal growth, and delineate the extent of what is acceptable and unacceptable within the relationship.

Boundaries exist in physical, emotional, mental, and even digital forms. Physical boundaries may relate to personal space, touch, and how one engages with their environment. Emotional boundaries involve understanding each person's emotional needs, vulnerabilities, and triggers. Mental boundaries could encompass respecting each other's thoughts, values, and opinions without imposing one's own. Digital boundaries could relate to using social media, sharing passwords, and respecting privacy in the digital realm.

Understanding these limitations is about knowing where they exist and respecting them in action. It's about giving each other the freedom to be separate individuals with unique needs, desires, and limitations. This respect often manifests in everyday choices—like asking for consent before making a decision that affects both parties or respecting each other's need for solitude or social interaction.

It's crucial to communicate these boundaries explicitly. Assuming that your partner knows your limitations without you expressing them is a recipe for misunderstanding. Open discussions about what makes each of you uncomfortable or what you find unacceptable can go a long way in preventing future conflicts.

However, setting boundaries doesn't mean creating emotional walls or promoting detachment. It's about finding a balanced way to engage with each other while maintaining individual integrity. It's akin to saying, "This is where I end, and you begin," which is essential for any form of healthy interdependence.

Additionally, boundaries are not static; they can change as individuals grow and the relationship evolves. What was acceptable at one stage in the relationship may become unacceptable later, and vice versa. Therefore, regular check-ins to reassess these boundaries are beneficial, especially during significant life changes like moving in together, getting married, or having children.

Understanding and respecting each other's boundaries and limitations fosters a relationship environment where both parties can thrive individually and as a couple. It prevents feelings of resentment, exploitation, or being overwhelmed, which are common pitfalls when boundaries are not well-defined or respected. In the grand scheme, a relationship with well-understood and respected boundaries will likely be more resilient, harmonious, and fulfilling for both parties involved.

UNDERSTANDING

Create New Memory Cards

The metaphor of creating a "new memory card" encapsulates the idea of intentionally choosing to start anew in the relationship, unburdened by past conflicts, misunderstandings, or disappointments. This is more than a mere emotional reset; it's a commitment to a future-oriented perspective that values growth and mutual happiness over dwelling on past grievances.

Why is this concept so critical in a relationship? Over time, the accumulation of small misunderstandings, minor grievances, and unresolved conflicts can weigh heavily on both partners. This baggage can subtly influence how you interact with each other, leading to a cycle of negativity that can be difficult to break. The concept of a "new memory card" is about breaking this cycle.

Creating a new memory card involves several steps. The first is a mutual acknowledgment of the need for a fresh start, usually through open communication. This is followed by a concerted effort to resolve or let go of past issues, either through dialogue, forgiveness, or possibly professional counselling.

Once this is achieved, the next step is to actively cultivate positive experiences and memories to "overwrite" the old, negative patterns. This could mean setting new relationship goals, planning shared activities, or even something as simple as expressing appreciation for each other more frequently.

Finally, maintaining this new memory card requires ongoing effort from both partners. It necessitates continual communication, regular check-ins on the relationship's emotional state, and a willingness to address and resolve conflicts promptly before they can fester and add new negative data to the memory card.

Addressing Needs, Wants, & Desires
Tools to Build Yourself and Others

1. **Empathy Exercises**: Practicing empathy can help you understand your partner's perspective, making conflicts more straightforward to resolve.
2. **Communication Workshops**: These can enhance your ability to express yourself clearly, reducing misunderstandings.
3. **Self-Improvement Books/Podcasts**: These resources can offer personal and relational growth insights.
4. **Counselling and Therapy**: Professional guidance can offer personalized strategies for understanding and growth.
5. **Journaling**: This can help you articulate and understand your feelings, which you can communicate more effectively to your partner.
6. **Ground Techniques**: Find some ways to ground yourself, avoiding your impulsive reaction to make a decision.
7. **Cognitive Behavioural Therapy**: Learn to have a positive, optimistic outlook on every situation.

Understanding yourself and your partner involves a deep dive into individual psychologies, emotional landscapes, and medical conditions that can affect behaviour and interaction. This comprehensive understanding forms the bedrock upon which a stable, fulfilling relationship can be built. It's an ongoing process requiring regular reassessment and adaptation, but the emotional and practical rewards are well worth the effort.

SOME MEN *THINK* DIFFERENTLY

Navigating a relationship is often likened to sailing a ship through waters that can sometimes be calm and, at other times, stormy. One of the most intricate aspects of this navigation is understanding how each person in the relationship thinks, processes emotions, and reacts to various situations. Often, this dynamic is further complicated by the inherent differences in how men and women typically approach problems, express emotions, and communicate. While avoiding painting entire genders with a broad brush due to individual differences and nuances is essential, recognizing some general tendencies can offer valuable insights. This chapter aims to explore these complexities and provide actionable advice for better mutual understanding.

The human brain is a marvel, an intricate organ that controls our bodily functions and our emotions, perceptions, and thoughts. The similarities and differences between male and female brains are not merely an academic curiosity; they have practical implications for how men and women interact with the world and, more importantly, with each other. Recognizing these cognitive and emotional variations is not a matter of declaring one superior to the other but is about understanding how they can complement each other in a relationship. After all, the beauty of a relationship often lies in the harmonious blending of two distinct individuals into a cohesive unit.

Emotions are crucial to human existence, colouring our experiences, shaping our reactions, and influencing our decisions. However, emotional expression and processing can vary between men and women, influenced by biological factors and social conditioning. Men are often taught from a young age to suppress emotions perceived as "weak," such as sadness or vulnerability. In contrast, women are generally encouraged to be more expressive about their emotional states. Understanding these different emotional languages is critical to a successful relationship, as it fosters empathy and opens the door for more effective communication.

In thought processes and problem-solving, men and women may employ different strategies. Some men are often described as more solution-focused, using logical and analytical reasoning to resolve issues quickly. Some women, on the other hand, may prioritize emotional context, valuing communication and mutual understanding over immediate resolution. These differences can be both a strength and a challenge in relationships. On the one hand, they provide a more comprehensive approach to problem-solving, combining rationality with emotional intelligence. On the other hand, they can be a source of conflict if not properly understood and managed.

This chapter will delve into various facets of these cognitive and emotional differences, examining them through the lens of neuroscience, psychology, and practical experience. We'll explore how these differences manifest in emotional reactions, problem-solving approaches, and communication styles. We'll also discuss the importance of achieving a balance between different cognitive and emotional styles, both within oneself and within the relationship. The goal is to provide a roadmap for better understanding between partners, enhancing the quality of the relationship by embracing and celebrating these differences rather than allowing them to become points of contention.

With that context set, let's dissect how these differences manifest in various aspects of a relationship, starting with the foundational differences in thinking between men and women.

How Do Some Men Think Differently Than Some Women?

The question of how men and women think differently has been the subject of extensive research and debate in psychology, neuroscience, and popular culture. While it's crucial to approach this topic with sensitivity to avoid reinforcing stereotypes or making overgeneralizations, some broadly observed trends can offer insights into common differences in male and female cognitive processes.

One of the most frequently cited differences is the approach to problem-solving. Some men often adopt a more linear, task-oriented strategy focused on finding solutions as efficiently as possible. This is not to say that men lack emotional depth or the ability to consider multiple aspects of a problem; instead, the inclination is toward directness and expediency in resolving issues. The cultural reinforcement of this trait—via social norms that encourage men to be decisive and action-oriented—can further accentuate this difference.

Some women, conversely, may approach problem-solving more holistically, considering emotional nuances and the impact of various outcomes on all parties involved. They are often more inclined to seek collaborative solutions that account for different perspectives. This isn't a matter of indecisiveness or overcomplication but a different cognitive strategy that places a higher value on emotional intelligence and interpersonal relationships.

Addressing Needs, Wants, & Desires

Another area where differences are often noted is in communication styles. Some men are generally taught to be less expressive about their emotions and may rely more on actions than words to convey their feelings or intentions. Some men may be more logical and factual driven than some women. They need reason and rationalization before making a decision. On the other hand, some women are typically socialized to be more emotionally expressive and verbally articulate in describing their feelings, thoughts, and concerns. This divergence in communication styles can sometimes lead to misunderstandings in relationships, particularly when each partner misinterprets the other's form of expression as either insufficiently emotional or overly analytical.

It's also worth noting that these differences are not just binary attributes tied to one's gender but exist along a spectrum influenced by a myriad of other factors, including but not limited to upbringing, cultural background, education, and personal experiences. Individual variances are the norm, and not every man or woman will conform to these observed patterns.

The key takeaway is that recognizing these general cognitive differences can offer valuable frameworks for understanding each other better. Still, they should not be used to pigeonhole or limit someone based on their gender. Understanding how your partner thinks—irrespective of whether these thought patterns align with broader gender trends—can foster better communication, reduce conflicts, and enrich mutual understanding.

What Does the Brain Have to Say About This?

The brain's role in explaining gender differences in thinking and emotional processing is a subject of considerable scientific interest and debate. While it's essential to be cautious about drawing sweeping conclusions, neuroscientific research has observed some structural and functional distinctions between male and female brains.

SOME MEN THINK DIFFERENTLY

The amygdala, a brain region linked with emotional processing, is generally more prominent in men. This has been interpreted to suggest that men might process emotions differently, possibly being more reactive to emotional stimuli. On the other hand, some women often show a more developed prefrontal cortex, the part of the brain associated with decision-making, problem-solving, and moderating social behaviour. This could explain why many women are often more adept at tasks requiring planning, organization, and multitasking.

Moreover, the connectivity patterns within the brain also appear to differ between genders. Some women may have more robust neural connections from side to side, potentially facilitating better communication between the analytical and intuitive parts of the brain. Some men, conversely, may have stronger connections from front to back, which might enhance their perception and motor skills.

However, it's crucial to emphasize several points here. Firstly, these are general trends, and there can be significant individual variation. Secondly, while brain structure can influence behaviour, it's only one part of a complex interplay of factors that include social conditioning, personal experiences, and environmental influences. The brain is highly plastic, meaning it can change and adapt, and this plasticity is influenced by a host of factors beyond biological sex.

Additionally, scientific understanding of this area is continually evolving. Early theories that sought to explain gender differences in terms of a single "male brain" or "female brain" have largely been discredited. The contemporary view is more nuanced, acknowledging that individual brains are a unique mosaic of features; some might be more common in one gender or the other, but many are distributed across a broad spectrum.

It is crucial to note that while understanding these neuroscientific observations can offer valuable insights, they should not be used to justify stereotyping, discrimination, or the reinforcement of traditional gender roles. Instead, this knowledge can serve as a tool for better mutual understanding, allowing couples to appreciate their differences and leverage their complementary strengths.

While the brain does offer some insights into how men and women might think differently, it's only a single piece of a much larger puzzle. Social, cultural, and individual factors are equally important, and a balanced perspective that considers all these offers the most accurate and constructive approach to understanding gender differences in relationships.

How Do Some Men React to Emotions?

It's essential to approach this topic with the understanding that emotional responses can vary widely among individuals, regardless of gender. However, societal norms and cultural conditioning often shape how men and women are "expected" to react to emotions.

Most men are frequently socialized from a young age to suppress certain emotions, particularly those perceived as vulnerabilities, including sadness, fear, or excessive joy. This social conditioning often falls under the broad umbrella of "masculinity," which can include a variety of traits but commonly emphasizes stoicism, strength, and emotional control. As a result of this socialization, men may be less likely to articulate their emotional states openly. Instead, they might choose to express themselves through actions rather than words or might opt to keep their emotional experiences private, even from close partners.

This tendency to be less expressive should not be confused with a lack of emotional depth or complexity. Some men experience emotions as intensely as some women but may have been conditioned to manage them differently. For example, where a woman might seek social support to process an emotional experience, a man might prefer to engage in a solitary activity to think things through. Alternatively, some men may channel their emotions into physical activity or immerse themselves in work or a hobby as a coping mechanism.

SOME MEN THINK DIFFERENTLY

The societal expectations placed on men to be "strong" can also have implications for how they react to their partner's emotions. When confronted with emotional issues, they may default to problem-solving mode, focusing on "fixing" the situation rather than exploring the emotional nuances. While this approach can be beneficial in specific contexts, it may not always meet the emotional needs of their partner, who might be looking for empathy and understanding rather than immediate solutions.

Understanding these general tendencies can be invaluable in a relationship, particularly for partners who may be puzzled by what they perceive as emotional distance or a lack of verbal or emotional expression. However, it's crucial to remember that each individual is unique. The most effective way to understand how any person, male or female, reacts to emotions is through open, honest, and non-judgmental communication. This enables both partners to express their emotional needs clearly and negotiate ways to meet those needs that respect both parties' comfort zones and emotional landscapes.

Why Some Women Can Be More Emotional Than Some Men?

The perception that women are more emotional than men is a topic that has been discussed and analyzed through various lenses, including psychology, neuroscience, and sociology. While it's crucial to avoid overgeneralizing or perpetuating gender stereotypes, specific research points to differences in emotional processing and expression between men and women.

Firstly, let's consider biological factors. More prevalent in women, hormones like estrogen and progesterone have been linked to emotional responsiveness. These hormones can influence mood and emotional reactivity, although the extent to which they do so can vary significantly from person to person. It's also worth noting that these hormones fluctuate throughout a woman's menstrual cycle, leading to varying degrees of emotional sensitivity at different times.

However, biology is just one piece of the puzzle. Sociocultural factors also play a significant role. From a young age, many societies socialize girls to be more expressive and communicative about their emotions. At the same time, boys may be taught to suppress emotional expression, particularly of emotions like vulnerability or sadness. This form of social conditioning can have long-lasting effects into adulthood, influencing how men and women engage with their emotions and those of others.

Emotional expression and emotional experience should be distinguished. While some women may be socialized to be more expressive about their emotions, this should not be conflated with experiencing emotions more intensely. Some men feel emotions just as profoundly but may express them differently due to societal norms or personal preferences.

The concept of emotional labour is also relevant here. Women often take on a disproportionate amount of emotional labour in relationships, which includes tasks like maintaining social calendars, remembering important dates, and even managing the emotional climate of the home. This additional emotional work can sometimes be mistaken as women being "more emotional" when, in fact, they are often just more involved in the emotional aspects of relationship maintenance.

It's important to note that emotional expressiveness should not be seen as a weakness. In fact, the ability to articulate and manage emotions contributes to greater emotional intelligence. Emotional intelligence, which involves recognizing, understanding, and managing not only one's own emotions but also the emotions of others, is invaluable in all kinds of relationships. It enhances empathy, improves conflict resolution, and fosters a deeper, more meaningful connection between partners.

SOME MEN THINK DIFFERENTLY

While there may be differences in how men and women typically handle emotions, these differences result from a complex interplay of biological, psychological, and sociocultural factors. Acknowledging and understanding this complexity can facilitate better communication and emotional understanding between partners, thereby enriching the relationship.

How To Balance the Three Minds?

The concept of balancing the "three minds" refers to an integrative approach to decision-making and emotional regulation, incorporating both emotional and rational elements to arrive at a balanced, or "wise," perspective. The Emotional Mind is driven predominantly by feelings, emotions, opinions, perceptions and impulses; it's the part of you that reacts viscerally to situations and is often the seat of your most immediate and raw emotional responses. It's the impulsive reaction to responding to people and situations. It is like a tomato, with thin skin on the outside but juicy on the inside.

Conversely, the Rational Mind operates based on logic, facts, reason, rationalization and objective analysis. It sets aside emotional influences to arrive at reasoned conclusions. The rational mind is like a cantaloupe, with thick skin on the outside but sweet on the inside.

The Wise Mind mediates these two, integrating emotional impulses with rational thought to achieve a balanced perspective. It thinks about the bigger picture, the future, and the best outcome for the now and the then. It's like an avocado. The skin is not too thin or thick, and the inside is just the perfect texture.

In the context of a relationship, balancing these three minds is particularly important because relationships often elicit strong emotional reactions while also requiring logical planning and decision-making. For instance, if your partner does something that upsets you, your Emotional Mind might want to react immediately, possibly in a way that could escalate the situation. Your Rational Mind, meanwhile,

Addressing Needs, Wants, & Desires

might step in to analyze the situation objectively, potentially leading you to suppress your emotional response entirely. The Wise Mind would help you navigate a middle path, allowing you to acknowledge and validate your emotional experience while considering the broader context and potential consequences of various responses.

Implementing this balance involves several steps:

1. **Self-Awareness**: The first step is recognizing which "mind" is predominating at any given moment. Are you reacting purely emotionally, or are you detaching yourself entirely and approaching the situation too analytically?
2. **Pause and Reflect**: Before reacting, especially in emotionally charged situations, take a moment to pause. This creates space for the Wise Mind to engage.
3. **Consult Both Minds**: Deliberately tap into both your emotional and rational sides. Validate your feelings without letting them control you, and analyze the situation without depersonalizing it entirely.
4. **Open Communication**: Share this balanced perspective with your partner. Use "I" statements to express your feelings and thoughts clearly and non-confrontationally.
5. **Mutual Understanding**: Encourage your partner to approach conflicts and decisions from a Wise Mind perspective. This reciprocal approach can lead to more effective problem-solving and greater emotional intimacy.
6. **Regular Check-ins**: Periodically review your decision-making and conflict-resolution patterns to see how well you're maintaining this balance. Make adjustments as needed.
7. **Seek External Input**: Sometimes, especially for significant decisions or persistent conflicts, external perspectives can be valuable. Whether it's advice from trusted friends or professional counselling, these viewpoints can help you better balance your Emotional and Rational Minds.

The application of the concept of the three minds can be a transformative tool in relationships. It allows for a nuanced approach to conflict resolution, enhances emotional intelligence, and fosters a deeper, more empathetic connection between partners. By actively working to balance your Emotional, Rational, and Wise Minds, you're investing in a foundational skill that can significantly contribute to the longevity and quality of your relationship.

Body Language and Non-Verbal Communication

Accurately interpreting body language and non-verbal cues is a crucial skill in understanding your partner's feelings, thoughts, and intentions. These non-verbal signals often convey a wealth of information that words alone cannot capture. It's not just about what is being said but also how it's being said, and what is being communicated through subtle physical expressions.

Facial expressions are one of the most immediate and telling forms of non-verbal communication. A smile, a frown, or a raised eyebrow can speak volumes about a person's emotional state or reaction to a situation. For instance, while a smile generally indicates happiness or approval, the absence of a smile during a typically joyful occasion could signal that something is amiss.

Eye contact is another powerful form of non-verbal communication. Steady eye contact usually signifies engagement and interest, while avoiding eye contact could indicate discomfort, dishonesty, or disinterest. The way eyes move can also be revealing; for example, frequent glances to the side might indicate distraction or evasion.

Posture and physical orientation are additional elements that provide clues about a person's feelings and attitudes. An open posture, where arms and legs are uncrossed, often indicates receptivity and openness to conversation. In contrast, a closed posture—such as crossed arms—may suggest defensiveness or a lack of openness.

Gestures, too, are a form of non-verbal communication that can range from grand, apparent movements to subtle shifts. A thumbs-up, a clenched fist, or a dismissive wave can effectively convey approval, anger, or rejection, respectively. Even subtle gestures like the tapping of fingers or weight shifting can indicate impatience or discomfort.

The tone, pitch, and volume of voice also carry non-verbal cues. A soft, low voice might indicate shyness or uncertainty, while a loud, high-pitched voice could reveal excitement or stress. The speed at which one talks can also be telling: rapid speech might be a sign of nervousness or excitement, whereas slow speech could signify careful thought or possibly disinterest.

It's important to note that cultural background can influence the meaning of body language. What is considered a positive or respectful gesture in one culture might have a different or even opposite meaning in another. Therefore, it's crucial to consider the cultural context when interpreting these cues.

Moreover, looking at non-verbal cues collectively rather than in isolation is essential to get a more accurate read of someone's feelings or intentions. For example, crossed arms might generally indicate defensiveness, but when paired with a smiling face and steady eye contact, the message could be quite different.

Reading body language and non-verbal communication is a skill that often requires time and keen observation to develop. However, the investment is worthwhile, as it can lead to a deeper understanding of your partner, better communication, and, consequently, a stronger relationship.

Roles and Responsibilities

The concept of roles and responsibilities within a relationship can be complex and nuanced, often shaped by a confluence of societal norms, cultural expectations, individual preferences, and practical necessities. Traditional models of relationships often delineated roles strictly based on gender, with men generally expected to be the primary earners and women expected to handle domestic responsibilities. However, contemporary relationships increasingly acknowledge the need for a more equitable and flexible approach to dividing roles and responsibilities between partners.

Roles in a relationship can encompass a broad range of functions, from financial management and career-related decisions to domestic chores, childcare, and emotional support. Responsibilities could also extend to social roles, such as how each partner represents the relationship within their respective social circles or families. The distribution of these roles and responsibilities is often a dynamic process, requiring ongoing communication and negotiation to ensure that both parties feel their needs are being met, and their talents are being effectively utilized.

It's crucial for partners to have open, honest conversations about their expectations regarding roles and responsibilities. This dialogue shouldn't be a one-time discussion but an ongoing conversation that evolves as the relationship progresses and circumstances change. For example, the birth of a child, a job change, or even a significant life event like an illness could necessitate a reevaluation of roles within the relationship.

Flexibility is critical in this context. Both partners should be willing to adapt and take on different responsibilities as needed. Rigid adherence to predefined roles can lead to dissatisfaction, resentment, and conflict. The aim should be to find a balance that suits both individuals, acknowledging that each will have their strengths, weaknesses, and preferences.

In an equitable relationship, roles and responsibilities are not just assigned but are agreed upon. Each person's comfort level, competencies, and aspirations should be considered in the distribution of roles. This mutual agreement helps to ensure that neither party feels exploited or overwhelmed, which can be detrimental to the long-term health of the relationship.

Addressing Needs, Wants, & Desires

Moreover, it's essential to review these roles and responsibilities periodically. Life stages change, as do personal and professional demands. What worked at one phase of the relationship may not be applicable later on. Regular check-ins can help reassess the suitability of the current arrangement and make necessary adjustments.

The assignment and acceptance of roles and responsibilities between two people in a relationship should be a collaborative, dynamic process. It should be rooted in mutual respect, open communication, and a willingness to adapt and change. This approach not only fosters a sense of partnership and equality but also contributes to the long-term success and satisfaction within the relationship.

Understanding the cognitive and emotional differences that often exist between men and women can be pivotal in relationship management. It allows for more empathetic engagement, better communication, and a deeper understanding of each other's needs and reactions. However, it's crucial to remember that these are general trends, and individual variations can be significant. Therefore, personalized communication and mutual understanding remain the most reliable tools for relationship success.

WANTS *AND* NEEDS

The complexity of human relationships often boils down to a simple yet intricate web of wants and needs. Although used interchangeably in casual conversation, these terms have profoundly different implications in personal relationships. As we move into the fifth week of this comprehensive guide, our focus shifts to understanding these differences, particularly how they manifest between men and women. Gender, of course, does not dictate the entirety of an individual's desires or necessities. Still, it offers a framework for exploration, one rooted in biological differences and social conditioning.

Acknowledging and understanding what each partner wants and needs can serve as the cornerstone for building a fulfilling, lasting relationship. It's not merely about meeting the basic needs for survival or even emotional well-being. Beyond that, it's about striving to create a partnership that accommodates each partner's desires and aspirations—those aspects that enrich life and make the journey more meaningful. However, aligning these wants and needs is rarely straightforward.

Addressing Needs, Wants, & Desires

The concepts of "want" and "need" are intrinsically tied to our experiences, expectations, and the roles we adopt or are assigned. They impact everything from our daily interactions to our long-term goals, and they can be as simple as the desire for shared leisure activities or as complex as the need for emotional security and mutual respect. Therefore, our approach must be nuanced, taking into consideration not just what we want and need individually but also what we can offer to meet our partner's wants and needs. This reciprocal understanding can enhance compatibility, reduce conflicts, and foster an environment where both partners can grow as individuals and as a couple.

This chapter aims to dissect these multifaceted issues systematically. We will begin by defining what constitutes a "need" versus a "want" before delving into how these categories often differ for men and women based on anecdotal evidence. But we don't stop at merely identifying these differences; the objective is to understand how we can bridge the gaps, find common ground, and build a balanced and fulfilling relationship. This involves compromise, but not where one side capitulates to the other. Instead, we aim for a form of compromise that respects the integrity and dignity of both partners, one that often leads to solutions neither could have envisioned alone.

Moreover, we will explore practical steps for achieving this harmonious balance. This includes actionable advice on how to communicate effectively about your wants and needs, how to negotiate successfully, and how to support each other in achieving individual and mutual goals. Finally, we will examine how to address and overcome the challenges that inevitably arise when two distinct individuals, each with their wants and needs, come together in a committed relationship.

With that comprehensive overview, let's embark on this crucial aspect of relationship-building, one that promises to turn a good relationship into a great one, marked by mutual respect, deep affection, and a shared vision for the future.

WANTS AND NEEDS

What Is the Difference Between a Need and a Want?

The concepts of "needs" and "wants" serve as critical pillars in the understanding of interpersonal relationships, and distinguishing between the two is paramount for relational harmony and personal well-being. In the most fundamental sense, a "need" refers to something essential for your survival, well-being, and overall functionality as a human being. These non-negotiable aspects of life form the bedrock of your mental, emotional, and physical health. Needs in a relationship might include trust, mutual respect, emotional support, and open communication. These foundational elements create a secure and enriching environment, allowing both partners to thrive.

"Wants," on the other hand, are elements that enhance your life but are not absolutely essential for your basic well-being. These could range from shared interests and hobbies to specific expectations about lifestyle choices, such as where to live or how to spend leisure time. For instance, you might "want" a partner who enjoys the same genre of movies, or you might "want" to dine out regularly as a couple. While these wants contribute to your happiness and make the relationship more enjoyable, they aren't fundamental to the relationship's viability.

Understanding the difference between needs and wants becomes particularly crucial when navigating challenges or conflicts. It helps prioritize what must be maintained for the relationship to continue and what can be adjusted or compromised. For example, if open communication is a "need," then that sets a boundary that should not be violated, such as lying or withholding critical information. On the flip side, if going out for a weekend adventure is a "want," it might be forgone under certain circumstances, like financial constraints or health issues, without jeopardizing the relationship's integrity.

Moreover, the difference between needs and wants is not static but can evolve over time and through different life stages. Early in a relationship, the "want" for constant companionship might feel like a "need," but as the relationship matures and both individuals grow, the ability to have independent time might become a new "need." Likewise, what starts as a "want" could evolve into a "need" depending on how the dynamics of the relationship unfolds or due to changes in external circumstances.

Therefore, regularly communicating about and reassessing these needs and wants is essential. Both partners should be clear about what they consider non-negotiable needs and what falls into the category of wants that can be compromised or adjusted. This mutual understanding serves as a roadmap for the relationship, guiding day-to-day interactions and long-term plans while providing a framework for conflict resolution.

What Is the Difference Between Men's Wants and Women's Needs?

The topic of men's wants, and women's needs differ in relationships. It should be approached with nuance, acknowledging that individual preferences can vary widely and that not all men or women fit into generalized patterns. However, some commonly observed tendencies, often influenced by a combination of social conditioning, psychological factors, and even biological predispositions, suggest that men and women may prioritize different aspects of relationships.

Men, for example, may often place a higher emphasis on aspects like sexual compatibility, shared activities, and companionship. These can be categorized as "wants" because they are things that men often desire to have in a relationship but may not see as absolute necessities for the relationship to exist. These "wants" can contribute to the overall quality and enjoyment of the relationship but might not be considered essential building blocks.

Conversely, women may prioritize elements like emotional connection, open communication, and a sense of security and commitment. These can be seen as "needs" because they often serve as foundational aspects upon which many women build their relationships.

WANTS AND NEEDS

In this context, "needs" are those non-negotiable elements that women require for the relationship to be considered viable and fulfilling.

It's crucial to note that these categories are not mutually exclusive. Men also have emotional needs, such as the need for respect, affirmation, and emotional intimacy, just as women have wants that extend beyond emotional connection, like sexual fulfillment and shared interests. The difference often lies in the weight or importance placed on these aspects.

It's also essential to consider the significant role that cultural, social, and individual factors play in shaping these preferences. Social conditioning from a young age can influence men to prioritize autonomy, problem-solving, and physical intimacy. At the same time, women may be conditioned to seek emotional closeness, verbal communication, and relational stability.

Understanding these general tendencies is helpful, not as rigid rules, but as frameworks that can help partners navigate the complexities of their relationship. Recognizing these patterns can lead to more insightful conversations between partners about their needs and wants, paving the way for a more fulfilling and harmonious relationship.

How Do We Meet Each Other in the Middle?

Meeting each other in the middle is a nuanced endeavour that carefully balances individual needs, wants, and expectations within the relational context. It's an ongoing process requiring continuous communication, emotional intelligence, and a willingness to compromise without sacrificing one's core needs or values. Essentially, it's the art of finding common ground in a landscape of diverse interests, preferences, and requirements.

The first step toward meeting in the middle is a clear, open dialogue about what each partner needs and wants from the relationship. This conversation should not be superficial; rather, it should delve

Addressing Needs, Wants, & Desires

deeply into individual aspirations, emotional needs, and even fears or concerns each person might have. The objective is to create a comprehensive picture of what each partner wants to achieve or experience within the relationship framework.

After openly communicating these needs and wants, the next step is the analytical process of identifying overlaps and divergences between both parties' expectations. Where are the commonalities? Where are the points of divergence that could potentially lead to conflict? Understanding these areas facilitates formulating a strategy to accommodate both partners' preferences to the extent possible.

Compromise is often used to bridge gaps between differing needs and wants. However, it's important to distinguish between healthy compromises and those that undermine one's well-being or core values. A healthy compromise is a mutual adjustment where both parties may give up part of what they want but still feel satisfied and respected. On the other hand, a compromise that results in one or both partners feeling dissatisfied, disrespected, or marginalized is counterproductive in the long term.

One effective method for reaching a compromise is the "give-and-take" approach, where each partner agrees to yield on some points in exchange for concessions on others. For example, if one partner values spending quality time at home and the other values social engagements, they might agree to designate certain days for social activities and others for staying in. The key is to find a balance that honours both partners' needs and wants without causing undue strain or resentment.

It's also crucial to revisit these agreements periodically. Relationships are dynamic, and individual needs and circumstances can change. What worked at one point may no longer be suitable, necessitating a new round of discussions and compromises.

Meeting each other in the middle is not a one-off event but a recurring requirement for maintaining a harmonious, fulfilling relationship. It requires each person to be attuned to their own needs and desires and those of their partner. Through continuous communication, mutual respect, and the artful negotiation of compromises, both partners can create a relationship where individual aspirations are acknowledged and collective goals are achieved.

How Do We Compromise and Compliment?

The notions of compromise and complementing each other in a relationship are closely interconnected, and both are instrumental in building a harmonious and fulfilling partnership. These two aspects allow couples to navigate differences, leverage strengths, and foster a sense of unity and shared purpose.

Compromise is often misconstrued as a loss or sacrifice, where one party gives up something for the benefit of the other. However, a more constructive way to view compromise is as a collaborative form of problem-solving. It's an exercise in empathy, understanding, and negotiation aimed at finding a middle ground that accommodates both individuals' fundamental needs and wants. The objective is not to 'win' but to arrive at a solution that minimizes dissatisfaction and promotes mutual respect and partnership.

Effective compromise starts with open and honest communication. Both parties must be willing to express their needs, desires, and concerns clearly. Once these are laid out, the next step is to prioritize them. Not all needs and wants are equally important, and recognizing which ones are non-negotiable and which are flexible is crucial.

After identifying and prioritizing needs and wants, the actual negotiation can begin. This may involve trade-offs, where one partner agrees to concede in one area in exchange for a concession in another. For example, if one partner values spending holidays with their family and the other prioritizes vacation time as a couple, a possible compromise could be alternating holiday plans each year.

Addressing Needs, Wants, & Desires

Complementing each other in a relationship refers to how partners can enhance each other's lives by bringing different strengths, perspectives, and skills to the table. Unlike compromise, which often deals with differences and potential points of conflict, complementing each other focuses on synergies. The idea is that each individual has unique strengths and weaknesses, and a well-matched couple will find that their strengths can help mitigate each other's weaknesses.

For instance, if one partner is particularly adept at handling finances, they might be responsible for managing the household budget. If the other partner excels in social interactions, they might lead in maintaining the couple's social calendar. This division of labour is not about pigeonholing each person into a specific role but rather about leveraging each individual's natural abilities to benefit the collective partnership.

But complementing each other goes beyond just functional aspects; it also extends into emotional and psychological dimensions. For example, a naturally optimistic person may help balance a partner who tends to worry, providing emotional support and a different perspective in challenging times.

Compromise and complementing each other are dynamic processes that require ongoing effort, communication, and adjustment. While compromise focuses on navigating differences and finding mutually acceptable solutions, complementing each other is about leveraging individual strengths to create a more extraordinary partnership than the sum of its parts. Both are vital for a relationship's long-term success and happiness, helping build a strong foundation based on mutual respect, understanding, and love.

How Do We Fulfill Each Other's Goals, Dreams, and Visions?

Fulfilling each other's goals, dreams, and visions within a relationship is an intricate process beyond mere verbal affirmation or superficial support. It's an active, ongoing commitment that manifests in various dimensions—emotional, psychological, financial, and even logistical. Each partner's personal or professional aspirations become shared objectives that both parties actively work toward, with the understanding that individual success contributes to collective happiness and well-being.

The first critical step in this process is profoundly understanding each individual's goals, dreams, and visions. This entails more than just casual conversations; it may involve formal discussions where each partner outlines their aspirations clearly. These could range from career advancements, educational pursuits, and financial milestones to personal growth objectives like physical fitness, spiritual development, or mastering a new skill.

Once these aspirations are clearly defined, the next phase involves formulating a realistic and achievable plan to reach them. This could mean setting a timeline, allocating resources, and determining what sacrifices or compromises may be required from both parties. For instance, if one partner aspires to go back to school for further education, this could involve financial planning to cover tuition fees and other expenses and adjustments in household responsibilities.

Emotional support is another crucial component. Pursuing a dream often comes with its share of challenges, setbacks, and moments of self-doubt. Being each other's emotional anchor during these times is invaluable. This emotional support can manifest in various ways, from providing a listening ear and constructive feedback to offering encouragement and validation.

Moreover, there are day-to-day practicalities to consider. For example, if one partner's job requires frequent travel or long hours, the other partner might take on more household responsibilities to facilitate this. Or, if one partner is pursuing a fitness goal, the other might join in not just for moral support but to make the process more enjoyable and mutually beneficial.

Addressing Needs, Wants, & Desires

It's also essential to continuously monitor progress and adapt plans as needed. Circumstances change, unexpected obstacles arise, and initial plans may need to be revised. Regular "check-in" discussions can be helpful to assess where each person is in their journey towards their goals and what adjustments are required to continue to support each other effectively.

Fulfilling each other's goals also implies a level of mutual accountability. Each partner should feel responsible for helping the other stay on track, which can involve gentle reminders, encouragement, or even occasional tough love when one person is veering off course.

Notably, while individual goals and dreams are crucial, having shared goals as a couple is also beneficial. These can be as simple as saving for a house or as complex as building a business together. Shared goals provide a common purpose and strengthen the relationship by requiring teamwork, cooperation, and mutual growth.

In essence, fulfilling each other's goals, dreams, and visions is not passive but an active, dynamic process that evolves. It requires open communication, meticulous planning, emotional support, practical adjustments, and a willingness to make sacrifices and compromises for the greater good of both the individual and the relationship. By taking these steps, you enrich each other's lives and build a stronger, more resilient partnership that is better equipped to face whatever challenges lie ahead.

How Do We Address Issues and Challenges in a Relationship?

Navigating issues and challenges is an unavoidable aspect of any relationship. These issues can range from minor disagreements to significant conflicts, and they may pertain to various topics such as finances, family planning, emotional support, or even individual habits and behaviours. Effectively addressing these challenges is essential for maintaining a healthy, balanced relationship, and it typically involves a multi-step approach.

The first step in resolving any problem is acknowledging that it exists. This may seem straightforward, but many issues go unaddressed simply because one or both parties are unaware or unwilling to acknowledge them. The identification phase may involve self-reflection, observation, or external feedback from friends, family, or professionals. It's crucial to approach this step without judgment and to be open to recognizing problems that may not align with your initial perceptions.

Once an issue has been identified, the next step is open, honest communication. This involves discussing the problem candidly but constructively, avoiding blame or personal attacks. The objective is to ensure both parties fully understand the issue and its implications. Effective communication often requires active listening skills, where you listen to understand rather than respond, and using "I-statements" to express feelings without making the other person defensive.

Understanding where each partner comes from is vital to the communication process. This involves listening to their words and understanding their emotions and motivations. It's about recognizing the legitimacy of each other's feelings and perspectives, even if you disagree. This step may require empathy, patience, and sometimes willingness to see the world through your partner's eyes.

After understanding each other's perspectives, the next stage is finding a middle ground—a compromise that respects both parties' needs and wants. Compromise doesn't mean one party giving in to the other but finding a solution that, while not perfect for either, is acceptable to both. This may involve negotiation, concessions, and sometimes, creative problem-solving to find alternative solutions that meet both parties' core needs.

Addressing Needs, Wants, & Desires

The final step in addressing issues is taking actionable steps to implement the agreed-upon solution. This could involve behavioural changes, setting new boundaries, or seeking external help such as counselling or financial planning. Monitoring the effectiveness of these changes is equally important, as it allows for adjustments and fine-tuning.

Sometimes, the challenges may be too complex or deeply rooted to resolve without professional assistance. In such cases, couples therapy or counselling can provide a neutral, structured environment for addressing issues. Therapists can offer expert guidance and tools for communication and problem-solving that can be invaluable in resolving conflicts.

Addressing issues and challenges effectively is not a one-off task but an ongoing process that evolves as the relationship grows and changes. Being proactive in identifying and tackling issues, being committed to open and respectful communication, and being willing to compromise and adapt are all essential for the long-term success and health of the relationship.

Understanding what each partner wants and needs is the cornerstone of a fulfilling relationship. It's about fulfilling basic needs and striving for a partnership that accommodates both partners' desires and aspirations. This process requires a balanced approach that combines open communication, mutual respect, and the willingness to compromise and adapt. By taking the time to understand and meet each other's wants and needs, you not only create a harmonious relationship but also set the stage for mutual growth and happiness.

CONFLICT **RESOLUTIONS**

Conflict is an inevitable aspect of any relationship. Conflicts, whether disagreements about household chores, differing opinions on finances, or deeper issues like trust and fidelity, will arise. While the presence of conflict is a given, navigating it can significantly impact your relationship's longevity, health, and overall satisfaction.

This chapter delves into the intricacies of conflict resolution, aiming to provide you with the tools you need to tackle big and small challenges. Understanding that conflict is not inherently negative, but a natural part of human interaction can help reframe how you approach disputes. Resolving conflicts effectively can strengthen your relationship and lead to a deeper understanding of each other.

It's essential to approach conflict resolution with a mindset focused on mutual understanding rather than winning or losing. This means actively listening to your partner's concerns, engaging in open and honest communication, and showing empathy even when disagreeing. The objective is not to prove yourself right but to find a solution that respects both parties' needs and wants. Compromise is

Addressing Needs, Wants, & Desires

often necessary, but it should never come at the expense of your core values or emotional well-being.

This chapter will guide you through various scenarios and issues that are familiar sources of conflict in relationships. From addressing minor annoyances that can accumulate over time to tackling significant issues head-on, you'll learn strategies to handle conflict constructively. We'll discuss how to communicate effectively, avoiding the pitfalls of becoming emotionally charged or taking things personally. You'll also learn how to create an environment that facilitates open dialogue, breaking down barriers that can lead to an "eggshell environment" or even more damaging behaviours like gaslighting.

Moreover, the chapter will explore the role of self-awareness and emotional intelligence in conflict resolution. Understanding your triggers and your partner's can provide valuable insights into why conflicts arise and how to de-escalate them. Techniques such as active listening and the use of "I-statements" will be explored in depth, providing you with practical tools to improve communication.

Additionally, we will consider the importance of professional help for conflicts that are particularly challenging to resolve independently. Sometimes, external perspectives from therapists or counsellors can provide invaluable insights and offer structured environments to address issues safely and constructively. Whether navigating the daily ups and downs of partnership or encountering significant roadblocks, the principles and tools outlined in this chapter aim to equip you with the skills needed to resolve conflicts in a healthy, respectful manner. By dedicating time and effort to improving your conflict resolution abilities, you're investing in your relationship's long-term success and emotional richness.

Challenging Relationship Questions

Addressing challenging questions in a relationship is an inevitable part of sharing your life with another person. Whether these

CONFLICT RESOLUTIONS

questions pertain to finances, trust, future plans, sexual or emotional needs, they often strike at the core of individual values and expectations. As such, these questions can provoke emotional reactions, making it easy to feel attacked or defensive. However, the ability to discuss these matters calmly and constructively is crucial for the long-term success and health of the relationship. Here are some detailed strategies on how to approach such situations:

Before entering into a conversation that you anticipate will be challenging, take some time to center yourself. Emotional regulation techniques, such as deep breathing, mindfulness, or even brief physical exercise, can help lower stress levels and prepare you for a more rational discussion. The objective is to engage your prefrontal cortex, the part of the brain responsible for analytical thinking, rather than allowing the emotional amygdala to take over.

Choose an appropriate time and setting for the discussion, free from distractions and interruptions. Usually, 30-40 minutes a week should suffice. Try not to log down the issues so that if you could not recall them on the day of the discussion, they were not as important as you thought. The idea is not to address the issues but to have a discussion. You may address an issue with your partner; however, your statement should be "How can **we** work on solutions?" or "What can **we** do to avoid this from happening again?" No pointing fingers at each other; if there are no solutions, postpone it for next week.

Ensure you and your partner have the time and emotional bandwidth to engage in a potentially heavy conversation. Setting the stage also means approaching the conversation with a specific intention—seeking understanding, finding a compromise, or simply expressing your feelings.

The use of active listening and the Socratic method can be highly effective. Active listening involves fully concentrating, understanding, and responding to what your partner is saying. It requires that you not only listen to the words but also catch the nuances and emotions behind them. The Socratic method involves asking open-ended questions to gain deeper insight into your partner's perspective. Instead of asking, "Why do you always do that?" you might ask, "Can you help me understand what goes through your mind when you make that choice?"

When presenting your side, use "I" statements to frame the conversation around your feelings and perceptions without blaming or accusing your partner. Instead of saying, "You never listen to me," say, "I feel unheard when you don't engage with what I'm saying." This approach makes it less likely that your partner will become defensive, facilitating a more constructive conversation.

Words like "always" and "never" are often inaccurate and serve to polarize positions. Stick to specific instances and avoid generalizing behaviour over time, which can escalate tensions and sidetrack the conversation.

Remember, the objective is not to "win" the argument but to reach a mutual understanding and find a solution that respects both parties' needs and wants. Sometimes, this might involve compromise; other times, it may mean agreeing to disagree respectfully.

After the discussion, take some time to reflect on what was said and what was resolved. It may also be helpful to have a follow-up conversation to check in on any agreements or compromises made to ensure they are being implemented and are effective.

By approaching challenging questions with emotional intelligence, open-mindedness, and effective communication strategies, you can turn potential conflicts into opportunities for deeper understanding and stronger relational bonds.

How Do You Address the Pebble in Your Shoe?

The metaphor of the "pebble in your shoe" aptly captures those minor annoyances or irritants in a relationship that, although small, can become surprisingly disruptive over time if not addressed. These might

CONFLICT RESOLUTIONS

include habits as innocuous as leaving dirty dishes in the sink or always running late. Still, their impact can be disproportional to their size, often triggering more extensive arguments or creating a sense of resentment. Addressing these "pebbles" is essential in relationship management, as it prevents minor issues from snowballing into significant problems.

The first step in addressing these minor irritants is communicating openly about them. This requires choosing an appropriate time and setting where both parties are not already stressed or distracted. The communication should be straightforward but tactful, framing the issue as something bothering you rather than as a fault in your partner. Using "I" statements can be effective here, as in, "I feel frustrated when the dishes are left in the sink."

It's crucial to approach the discussion without assigning blame. The objective is not to accuse your partner but to express how a specific action impacts you. Focus on the behaviour, not the person. The idea is to present it as an observation that leads to a feeling, thereby giving your partner the space to respond without becoming defensive.

Being vague won't help resolve the issue. Clearly define what the annoyance is and how it makes you feel. Offering a solution can also be beneficial, shifting the focus from the problem to collaborative problem-solving. For instance, if the issue concerns dirty dishes, a possible solution could be, "Could we make it a routine to clean the dishes immediately after dinner?"

Addressing minor annoyances is a two-way street. If you're pointing out a pebble in your shoe, be prepared for your partner to mention their pebbles. The goal is a healthier, more comfortable relationship for both parties, which may mean addressing more than one issue.

Once you've discussed and ideally resolved the minor annoyance, it's helpful to have regular check-ins to ensure the issue has been fully addressed and isn't resurfacing. This also offers an opportunity to discuss any new "pebbles" that may have appeared, maintaining open communication channels.

It's essential to recognize that not every pebble needs to be removed. Some minor annoyances may be permanent characteristics of your partner that you need to accept. Knowing when to address an issue and when to let it go is part of developing a mature, resilient relationship.

By taking a proactive, communicative approach to address the "pebbles" in your relationship, you not only resolve minor irritations before they become significant issues but also develop invaluable communication and problem-solving skills that will benefit you in tackling more significant challenges.

Addressing the Elephant in the Room

Addressing significant and often uncomfortable issues—commonly referred to as "the elephant in the room"—is critical for the health and longevity of any relationship. These issues can range from lies and infidelity to emotional affairs and past relationships with the opposite sex or sexual lifestyle. Addressing these issues is often complicated and fraught with emotional volatility, which is why they frequently go unaddressed, leading to long-term damage.

The first step in addressing the elephant in the room is choosing an appropriate time and setting for the conversation. This should be a space where both parties can speak freely without distractions or interruptions. Timing is also crucial; it's best to choose a moment when both parties are calm and have the emotional bandwidth to tackle complex topics. Springing these conversations on your partner unexpectedly can lead to defensiveness and conflict.

Before diving into the conversation, it can be helpful to prepare what you want to say. Outline the key points you wish to discuss and consider the language you will use. The aim is to frame the conversation in a non-confrontational way that focuses on constructive outcomes.

CONFLICT RESOLUTIONS

Employ "I-statements" to express your feelings without blaming or accusing your partner. For example, say, "I feel hurt when I think about your past relationship," instead of "You hurt me with your past relationship."

During the discussion, it's crucial to employ active listening. This involves not only hearing the words your partner is saying but also understanding the emotions and motivations behind them. Emotional intelligence plays a significant role here, allowing you to navigate your emotions while being sensitive to your partner's feelings. This approach can distinguish between a constructive discussion and a heated argument.

One of the primary objectives in these difficult conversations is understanding your partner's perspective. This means asking open-ended questions and giving them space to express themselves. It might be challenging to hear some of their responses, but understanding the "why" behind their actions or feelings is crucial if you're seeking to resolve the issue genuinely.

Once the issue has been entirely laid out and both parties have had the chance to speak, the next step is discussing potential solutions or outcomes. This could range from setting new boundaries to seeking professional help through relationship counselling. The key here is to find a resolution that both parties can agree on, understanding that it may require compromise or sacrifice from both sides.

The conversation shouldn't end once a potential solution has been identified. It's crucial to have follow-up discussions to assess whether the agreed-upon changes are working or if further adjustments are needed. Accountability is critical here; both parties must be willing to take responsibility for their actions moving forward.

There are instances where the issue is too complex or sensitive to handle without professional guidance. Couples therapy can offer a structured environment for tackling these elephants in the room in cases involving infidelity, emotional abuse, or deeply ingrained behavioural issues. Therapists can provide neutral mediation and professional strategies for resolution that might be difficult to achieve otherwise.

Addressing the elephant in the room is complex but necessary for maintaining a healthy relationship. It requires careful planning, emotional intelligence, open communication, and sometimes professional intervention. While initiating these conversations is often uncomfortable, failing to do so can lead to long-term damage and resentment, undermining the relationship's very foundation. Therefore, it is in the best interests of both parties to face these issues head-on, with honesty, understanding, and a commitment to finding a resolution.

Addressing Icing (Being Cold, Walking Away, Not Addressing the Issues, etc.)

The phenomenon of "icing" in a relationship refers to emotionally distant or avoidant behaviours that serve as a barrier to meaningful communication and conflict resolution. This can manifest in several ways: one partner may become emotionally unavailable, physically remove themselves from difficult conversations, or simply refuse to engage in discussions that address underlying issues in the relationship. These actions can create a chilling effect, discouraging open dialogue and leaving problems unaddressed.

Understanding the underlying reasons for "icing" behaviours is crucial for effective resolution. These reasons vary widely, from a fear of confrontation or vulnerability to a lack of emotional investment in the relationship. In some cases, icing may be a learned behaviour, a coping mechanism developed from past relationships or childhood experiences. Identifying the root cause often involves introspection and, in many cases, open dialogue with your partner, possibly facilitated by a relationship counsellor.

If you decide to address the issue directly, choosing an appropriate time and setting is essential. Confronting your partner about their emotionally distant behaviour during a stressful moment will unlikely yield a productive conversation. Instead, choose a time when both parties are calm and can focus on the discussion. The setting should be private and free from distractions, creating a safe space for honest communication.

When discussing the issue, employ effective communication techniques to ensure that both parties can express themselves openly. Use "I-statements" to describe your feelings and experiences without assigning blame. For example, say, "I feel hurt and ignored when you walk away from our conversations," rather than "You hurt me by walking away." Active listening skills can also be invaluable, where you listen to understand rather than respond.

Professional intervention may be necessary if direct communication doesn't resolve the issue or if the icing behaviour is a symptom of a more significant underlying problem. A trained therapist can help identify the root causes of emotional distancing and provide strategies for improving communication and emotional intimacy. Couples therapy offers a neutral, structured environment where both parties can explore their feelings and behaviours under the guidance of a professional.

Failing to address icing behaviours can have long-term detrimental effects on a relationship. Over time, the lack of open communication can lead to a build-up of resentment, misunderstandings, and emotional detachment. This can erode the trust and intimacy that are the foundation of a healthy relationship, potentially leading to its eventual breakdown.

Addressing icing is not just about confronting the behaviour but also about building emotional resilience within the relationship. This involves developing the skills and emotional intelligence to navigate difficult conversations without resorting to avoidant behaviours. Both partners must be committed to fostering an emotional environment where open dialogue is encouraged and concerns are addressed promptly and constructively.

Addressing "icing" behaviours in a relationship is a complex but necessary task. It requires a multi-faceted approach, combining self-awareness, open communication, and possibly professional help. Both partners must be willing to engage in this process to resolve the immediate issue and build the emotional skills that will prevent similar problems in the future.

Addressing the Eggshell Environment

Walking on eggshells, or navigating an "eggshell environment," is commonly used to describe a situation where one or both partners in a relationship feel they must tread carefully to avoid triggering conflict, anger, or emotional volatility. This constant state of heightened caution can be emotionally draining and is often indicative of underlying issues that may range from fear of confrontation, emotional abuse, manipulation, or a general lack of emotional safety and trust within the relationship.

The first step in addressing this type of environment is identifying the underlying issues that contribute to it. Is it a fear of confrontation from past experiences, either within this relationship or from previous relationships? Is it a symptom of emotional or psychological abuse, where one partner uses manipulation or intimidation to control the other? Or could it be an issue of mistrust, where past betrayals or dishonesty have led to a lack of emotional safety? Pinpointing the root cause is crucial for effective resolution. It may require introspection, open dialogue, and possibly professional intervention.

Once the root cause has been identified, the next step is to initiate an open and honest conversation about the issue. This dialogue should ideally occur at a time and place where both parties can speak freely and focus on the conversation. Ground rules may need to be set to ensure

CONFLICT RESOLUTIONS

constructive dialogue, such as agreeing to avoid blame, name-calling, or raising past issues that are not directly related to the current problem. The objective is to explore the reasons behind the eggshell environment and to discuss ways to create a more secure emotional space for both partners.

In some instances, especially when the issue involves emotional or psychological abuse, professional help may be necessary. Therapists or counsellors can provide a neutral setting and expert guidance to navigate the complexities of the issue. They can offer tools and strategies to improve communication, rebuild trust, and enhance emotional safety, thereby dismantling the eggshell environment.

After identifying the root cause and discussing potential solutions, the next step is implementation. This could involve changes in behaviour, communication styles, or even the setting of new boundaries. Both parties should commit to these changes and regularly monitor their effectiveness. An open dialogue should continue to ensure that the implemented changes lead to a more emotionally safe and trusting environment.

The process of addressing an eggshell environment is not a one-time event but an ongoing process. Regular check-ins are essential to evaluate the changes' effectiveness and make necessary adjustments. Life circumstances change, and the relationship will evolve, requiring continuous efforts to maintain an emotionally safe space.

Addressing an eggshell environment is a complex but crucial aspect of sustaining a healthy relationship. It requires concerted effort, open communication, and sometimes professional intervention. The objective is to create a relationship where both parties can express themselves freely without fear of undue conflict or emotional upheaval. Proactively addressing the factors contributing to an eggshell environment lays the foundation for a more emotionally secure, trusting, and ultimately fulfilling relationship.

Addressing Gaslighting

Gaslighting is a form of psychological manipulation in which one person seeks to sow doubt in another, making them question their memory, perception, or judgment. It is a complex and harmful behaviour that can profoundly impact a relationship, undermining trust, emotional well-being, and even the victim's sense of reality. Addressing gaslighting is crucial and challenging because of its insidious nature and the severe emotional toll it can take.

The first step in confronting gaslighting is recognizing its signs, which are often subtle and easily dismissed. These might include contradictory statements, denial of previous conversations, or actions that intentionally confuse the victim. The gaslighter may also employ tactics like belittling, trivializing the victim's feelings, or shifting blame to evade accountability. Being alert to these signs is essential because gaslighting can be so effective that victims may start doubting their perceptions.

In some cases, gathering evidence of the gaslighting behaviour may be helpful. This could be in the form of text messages, emails, or even audio recordings. Collecting evidence serves a dual purpose: it can provide a point of reference for the victim to trust their perceptions and serve as a concrete basis for discussion or therapy.

Once gaslighting has been identified, it's crucial to set clear boundaries. This involves directly confronting the gaslighter about their behaviour and stating unequivocally what is unacceptable. However, setting boundaries can be particularly challenging in a gaslighting scenario because the gaslighter may use manipulation tactics to avoid taking responsibility. Therefore, strong resolve and external support are often needed to enforce these boundaries effectively.

Due to the emotionally damaging nature of gaslighting, external support is often vital. This could come from trusted friends and family or professionals like psychologists or counsellors. A support network can provide emotional sustenance, validation, and practical advice on handling the situation.

Because of the severe emotional and psychological impact of gaslighting, professional intervention is often necessary. Therapists can provide a safe space to explore the victim's feelings and perceptions and offer coping strategies. In couples therapy, the therapist can serve as a neutral third party to facilitate communication between the victim and the gaslighter. However, it's important to note that therapy can be ineffective or counterproductive if the gaslighter is unwilling to acknowledge and change their behaviour.

In extreme cases, legal action may be required, especially if the gaslighting accompanies other forms of abuse. Legal remedies can range from restraining orders to more severe criminal charges, depending on the case's jurisdiction and specifics.

Addressing gaslighting is a complex process that often requires a multifaceted approach, including self-empowerment, external support, and professional intervention. Due to the deep emotional and psychological scars that gaslighting can inflict, handling it with the seriousness it deserves is crucial. The aim is to restore the victim's trust in their perceptions and rebuild the emotional foundations of the relationship, provided both parties are committed to change. If the gaslighter is unwilling or unable to change their behaviour, the victim may need to consider whether the relationship can continue in a healthy and respectful manner.

How Do We Collaborate?

Collaboration within a relationship is a multi-layered process that goes beyond merely existing together; it involves actively working in concert to enhance the quality of the relationship and achieve shared objectives. This collaborative approach can apply to various life facets— emotional support, household responsibilities, financial planning, or parenting.

Addressing Needs, Wants, & Desires

The cornerstone of effective collaboration is open, transparent communication. Both partners must feel safe expressing their thoughts, concerns, and desires without fear of judgment or reprisal. This communication is not a one-time event but an ongoing dialogue that evolves as the relationship progresses. Depending on what works best for both parties, it may involve formal discussions, casual conversations, or even written communication like lists or plans.

Respect is another critical component of collaboration. This means valuing each other's opinions, acknowledging each other's contributions, and showing appreciation regularly. Mutual respect sets the stage for a balanced relationship where both partners can express themselves freely and work together effectively.

Every individual brings a unique set of skills and strengths into a relationship. Recognizing and using these attributes can make tasks easier and more enjoyable for both parties. For example, suppose one partner is better at budgeting and finances. In that case, they might take on the responsibility of managing the household budget, while the other, who might excel at cooking, could take charge of meal planning and preparation.

In any collaboration, compromise is often necessary because no two people will agree on everything. The ability to make concessions or adjustments in your behaviour or expectations is crucial for collaborative success. It is not about one partner bending to the will of the other but finding a middle ground that respects both individuals' needs and wants.

As life evolves, so do relationships. Being adaptable and open to change is essential for long-term collaborative success. Whether it's a job change, the birth of a child, or entering retirement, each life stage brings its own set of challenges and opportunities for collaboration.

While utilizing each other's strengths is essential, offering support in areas where your partner may not be as strong is equally essential. Offering assistance or taking over specific tasks can provide emotional relief and strengthen the relationship bond.

How Do You Dance During a Storm?

"Dancing during a storm" metaphorically encapsulates how couples navigate difficult times or challenges in their relationships. The key components to successfully weathering these storms are resilience, emotional intelligence, and effective communication.

Resilience is the ability to bounce back from adversity. In the context of a relationship, this means not allowing setbacks or challenges to define you or your partnership. Resilient couples can face difficulties head-on and become more assertive on the other side.

Emotional intelligence involves recognizing, understanding, and managing your emotions and your partner's. It allows you to approach conflicts or challenges with empathy and understanding rather than defensiveness or aggression. High emotional intelligence can facilitate more effective communication and problem-solving, even in the heat of the moment.

During turbulent times, effective communication becomes even more critical. This means speaking your mind and actively listening to your partner. It involves asking open-ended questions to understand their point of view and employing active listening skills to ensure you fully grasp what they're saying.

Successfully "dancing during a storm" involves a delicate balance between addressing the immediate issue and maintaining the relationship's overall health. It's easy to get lost in the problem and forget the bigger picture. Reminding yourselves of the love, respect, and mutual goals that form the foundation of your relationship can provide the perspective needed to navigate through challenges.

Offering a listening ear, providing emotional support, and showing empathy are crucial during hard times. Sometimes, solutions may not be immediately apparent, but the act of being there for each other can, in itself, be a powerful stabilizer during storms.

By mastering the art of collaboration and learning how to navigate challenges effectively, couples can build a more resilient and fulfilling relationship. These skills don't develop overnight but require ongoing effort, communication, and a mutual commitment to growing as individuals and as a partnership.

Conflict Resolution Tips

1. **Active Listening**: Focus on understanding your partner's perspective before responding.
2. **Open and Honest Communication**: Clearly state your feelings, needs, and concerns without blaming or criticizing your partner.
3. **Seek to Understand Before Being Understood**: Try to understand your partner's point of view before pushing your own.
4. **Take Timeouts**: If a conversation gets too heated, it's okay to take a break and return to the discussion later.
5. **Use "I" Statements**: Frame the conversation regarding your experiences and feelings to avoid making your partner defensive.
6. **Seek Professional Help**: Don't hesitate to consult a therapist or counsellor for more severe or persistent issues.

Conflict resolution is an essential skill in any relationship. It involves the ability to resolve issues as they arise and the foresight to prevent potential problems through open communication, collaboration, and mutual respect. By effectively addressing both minor annoyances and significant challenges, you lay the groundwork for a resilient, fulfilling relationship.

ADDRESSING ISSUES

The past is a powerful influence, shaping our perceptions, expectations, and behaviours in the present. As we navigate the intricate dynamics of relationships, the past often rears its head, sometimes subtly and sometimes overtly, affecting how we connect with our partners. Addressing these historical factors—personal past experiences or collective societal norms—is imperative in forging a strong, healthy, and lasting relationship. It's not just about confronting the ghosts of relationships past but also about acknowledging the deeply ingrained habits, behaviours, and expectations that each of us brings into a partnership.

This chapter will tackle the complex and often sensitive issue of how the past influences our current relationships. We will delve into how previous emotional or psychological wounds can linger and impact our ability to connect with a new partner. How do we prevent these scars from becoming stumbling blocks in a new relationship? How do we heal old wounds so they don't bleed into new connections?

We'll also explore the aftermath of significant life events like divorce or separation from a previous relationship. Dissolving a

Addressing Needs, Wants, & Desires

marriage or a long-term relationship often leaves us with emotional baggage that can manifest as trust issues, commitment phobias, or other problems. How do we make peace with these events to give a new relationship the fresh start it deserves?

Furthermore, we'll look at the role of addiction in relationships. Addiction is a complicated issue with far-reaching impacts, affecting not only the individual grappling with it but also their loved ones. Whether it's substance abuse or something less tangible like pornography, addiction brings unique challenges to a relationship, requiring specialized strategies for both partners.

Then there's the issue of co-parenting. When children from previous relationships are part of the equation, additional layers of complexity emerge. Navigating these waters requires a balance of respect, understanding, and most importantly, open communication.

We'll round off the chapter by discussing something seemingly simple but incredibly contentious: the division of household chores. Who does what around the house may appear trivial, but it's often a flashpoint for deeper issues around fairness, respect, and equality in a relationship.

In each section, we'll provide actionable tools and tips to help you navigate these complex issues. The aim is to offer a comprehensive guide for addressing the multifaceted ways the past can influence your current relationship. By actively confronting these issues, you better understand yourself and learn to form more meaningful, resilient connections with others. With the right tools and mindset, you can turn your past experiences into invaluable lessons rather than let them become obstacles in your path to a fulfilling relationship.

As we delve into these topics, remember that self-awareness and open communication are your greatest allies. The goal is not to forget the past but to understand it so thoroughly that it loses its power to negatively impact your present and future. So, let's begin this deep exploration by first looking at how to address past hurt affecting your current relationship.

ADDRESSING ISSUES

Addressing Past Hurt (Pre-Relationship)

Navigating the complexities of past emotional or psychological wounds is a delicate process that requires comprehensive attention, both individually and as a couple. These past hurts can manifest in numerous ways, including but not limited to trust issues, anxiety, emotional unavailability, or even adverse reactions to specific situations that remind you of past experiences.

The initial stage of addressing past hurt typically involves self-work, where the individual takes the time to delve into their past, possibly with the aid of professional counselling or therapy. This is an introspective process aimed at understanding the source of the hurt, its triggers, and how it has shaped your emotional landscape. Individual work can help you develop coping mechanisms and emotional tools that allow you to deal with your past without letting it dictate your current behaviour.

Once you've gained some understanding and control over your past issues, involving your partner in the process is essential. This is best done through open, honest, and non-judgmental communication. The idea is not to burden your partner with your past but to give them the context they need to better understand your actions, reactions, and emotions. This understanding can be pivotal in avoiding misunderstandings and conflicts in the relationship.

After the issue has been laid out and discussed, the next step is to develop joint coping strategies. These could range from mutually agreed-upon ways to handle specific situations that may trigger past hurt to general methods of providing emotional support when needed. The goal is to cultivate a supportive, empathetic environment where both partners feel emotionally safe and secure.

As the relationship evolves, it may be necessary to revisit the issue and adjust your coping strategies. This is particularly true for long-term relationships that may undergo various life changes, such as moving, returning to school, changing jobs, or having children. These changes can present new triggers or challenges that require reassessing your coping mechanisms.

In cases where past hurt significantly impacts your current relationship, ongoing professional support may be necessary. Couples therapy can provide a neutral, structured environment for addressing these issues and offer expert guidance for developing coping strategies. Some couples find it beneficial to attend therapy individually and together to tackle the issue from all angles.

Addressing past hurt is not a quick fix but a continuous process that may require adjustments over time. By taking a proactive approach that includes individual self-work, open communication with your partner, and the development of joint coping strategies, you create a foundation for a relationship that's resilient to the challenges posed by past emotional and psychological wounds.

Addressing Divorce and Separation

When a person enters a new relationship carrying the weight of a previous marriage or long-term partnership that ended in divorce or separation, it's like walking into a new chapter of life with a backpack full of experiences, some of which may be painful or complicated. The emotional residue from past relationships can include a wide array of feelings like distrust, insecurity, fear of commitment, or even guilt. While these feelings are natural, they can cast a shadow over the new relationship if not appropriately addressed.

Open and honest dialogue is crucial for both partners to understand the emotional landscape they're navigating. This doesn't mean dwelling on every detail of the past but instead sharing the key emotional takeaways that might influence present behaviour or expectations. The aim is to ensure that past experiences do not unfairly burden the new relationship but also to acknowledge that the past has shaped who you both are today. This discussion can help to reset expectations and set new ground rules for the relationship.

Another vital aspect is giving yourself the time and emotional space to heal. Jumping into a new relationship before you've had time to process the end of a previous one can lead to a "rebound," which is usually not the best foundation for a lasting partnership. Healing might also involve forgiving yourself and your ex-partner for the failures and disappointments of the past. Forgiveness here isn't about absolving someone of their mistakes but rather freeing yourself from carrying the emotional baggage of past grudges into your new relationship.

For those who have children from previous relationships, the complexities multiply. Navigating the waters of blended families requires excellent tact, respect, and open communication. It's not just about you and your new partner; it's also about the children who have to adjust to a new family dynamic. Being sensitive to their needs while balancing the demands of a new relationship can be challenging. Legal considerations like custody arrangements must also be factored into the relationship dynamic, adding another layer of complexity.

In short, addressing divorce and separation from previous relationships in a new partnership involves a multi-faceted approach. It requires emotional openness, mutual respect, ample time for healing, and a solid commitment to starting anew while understanding that you both bring your histories to the table. This considered approach can lay a solid foundation for a new, healthier relationship, unencumbered by the ghosts of relationships past.

Addressing Addiction Issues

Addressing addiction issues in a relationship is a complex and emotionally charged endeavour that often necessitates a multidisciplinary approach involving medical, psychological, and social support mechanisms. The first critical step in this process is recognizing and acknowledging the existence of an addiction problem. This acknowledgment must be both individual and collective regardless of addiction, which may include substance abuse, illicit drugs, cannabis, pornography, food, shopping, social media, socializing, vacationing,

Addressing Needs, Wants, & Desires

financial investing, workaholic and procrastination, to name a few. The person struggling with addiction must admit to the issue, and the couple must jointly accept that this is a challenge they must face together. Once the problem is openly acknowledged, formulating a comprehensive action plan becomes the next priority. This plan may include an array of interventions such as specialized therapy, counselling, and possibly medical treatment like detoxification or medication for substance abuse disorders.

The role of the non-addicted partner in this process is nuanced and essential. Support from this partner can be a significant motivating factor for the addicted individual to seek and continue treatment. However, it's crucial to differentiate between being supportive and enabling the addiction. Enabling behaviours, such as making excuses for the addicted partner's actions or overlooking the addiction's consequences, can perpetuate the problem and hinder recovery. Therefore, setting clear boundaries and expectations is essential. This may involve hard decisions, like insisting on treatment as a condition for continuing the relationship or placing limits on financial or emotional support until the addicted partner seeks help.

The couple may also benefit from involving their immediate social support network, including friends and family, who can offer additional emotional support and practical assistance. Support groups, either for the addicted individual or for partners of addicted individuals, can provide valuable perspectives and coping strategies. Sometimes, the journey to recovery is long and fraught with setbacks, making the emotional toll on both partners significant. Thus, both individuals may benefit from individual or joint counselling to manage stress, improve communication, and strengthen their emotional well-being.

Addressing addiction is not just about treating the addicted individual but about recalibrating the relationship. This often requires both partners to adapt to new dynamics, such as shifts in power and responsibility, changes in lifestyle and social activities, and a renewed focus on open communication and mutual support. Given the complex

ADDRESSING ISSUES

and often persistent nature of addiction issues, professional intervention is usually advised for the best chances of long-term success.

Addressing Porn Addictions

Addressing porn addiction in a relationship is a delicate and often emotionally charged issue that can profoundly affect intimacy and trust between partners. While the subject might be difficult to broach, the first crucial step in tackling this problem is opening the lines of communication. Both partners must be honest about how the addiction affects them personally and the relationship. The person facing the addiction must be willing to acknowledge the issue, and the other partner should strive to approach the subject without judgment or blame, as difficult as that may be.

Once the issue is out in the open, seeking professional help is often the most effective next step. Therapists or counsellors specializing in addiction can offer targeted treatment options, including Cognitive Behavioral Therapy, medications, or a combination. It's important that both partners engage in the therapeutic process. While the individual with the addiction needs to understand the psychological or emotional triggers that lead to their behaviour, the partner also needs to comprehend the underlying issues that may be contributing to the addiction, whether it's emotional distance, lack of intimacy, or other relationship challenges. This dual involvement in treatment helps address the addiction's impact on the relationship.

The path to recovery is often long and fraught with setbacks. Patience and ongoing support are critical, but it's also essential for the non-addicted partner not to slip into the role of an enabler. This means setting clear boundaries and expectations, such as insisting on continued therapy or other treatment as a condition for maintaining the relationship. Both parties should seek support from trusted friends, family, or support groups throughout this process. These external support systems can provide additional emotional support and practical advice as the couple navigates the complexities of addiction within their relationship.

While challenging, addressing porn addiction presents an opportunity for growth and increased intimacy in a relationship. Through open dialogue, professional help, and a commitment to making changes, many couples can overcome this issue and emerge with a stronger, more trusting relationship.

Addressing Co-Parenting

Co-parenting in a relationship, especially when it involves children from previous relationships, is a complex yet rewarding endeavour that requires a unique blend of communication, understanding, and diplomacy. It's a continuous process that starts with open conversations about your parenting philosophies, your expectations, and your respective roles in your children's lives. In this context, it's crucial to acknowledge and respect any legal agreements or custody arrangements that might be in place, as these are non-negotiable factors that set the stage for how you will function as a blended family.

One of the vital aspects of successful co-parenting is presenting a united front. Even though you may not agree on every minor detail of child-rearing, it's essential for the children to see you working together cooperatively. This unity provides a sense of stability and security, which is beneficial for their emotional development. Your aim should be to create an environment where all children, regardless of whether they are biologically related to both adults in the household, feel equally loved, protected, and attended to.

However, establishing this balanced environment is not a task that falls on one person's shoulders; it's a mutual responsibility. Each partner should recognize and respect the other's role in the family dynamic. For example, suppose one partner has more experience with children or better skills in certain aspects of parenting. In that case, it's beneficial for the other partner to acknowledge this expertise and defer to it when appropriate. Likewise, suppose one parent has been primarily

ADDRESSING ISSUES

responsible for certain aspects of a child's care. In that case, the other parent should respect that established routine while gradually integrating themselves in the least disruptive way to the child's life.

Another essential element of co-parenting is flexibility. As children grow, their needs and schedules change, and the co-parenting arrangement must be adaptable enough to accommodate these changes. This might mean revisiting the terms of your initial agreement and making necessary adjustments. Such adaptations could include re-evaluating time spent with each parent, re-assigning responsibilities in line with evolving work commitments, or even introducing new traditions that incorporate all blended family members.

Co-parenting is a complex task involving high emotional intelligence, adaptability, and mutual respect. You and your partner undertake a journey together, guided by a shared vision for your family's well-being. Effective co-parenting is not just about dividing responsibilities or adhering to a schedule; it's about creating a harmonious, loving environment where every family member, regardless of their biological or legal ties, feels like an integral part of the whole.

Addressing the Chore List

Determining who handles which household chores is an aspect of relationship dynamics that may seem mundane but can have far-reaching implications for the quality and longevity of the relationship. This decision-making process should be inclusive and collaborative, involving both partners in open discussion and negotiation. Factors to consider include each person's skill set, personal preferences, and availability, given other commitments like work schedules or educational pursuits.

This collaborative approach is a departure from historical norms where traditional gender roles often predetermined who would handle tasks such as cooking, cleaning, laundry, paying bills, finances, grocery shopping, taking care of the children, mechanical work, household chores, and yard work, to name a few. Modern relationships strive for a more equitable distribution, recognizing that both partners contribute to the household and should have a say in its upkeep.

The objective of this conversation is not just the division of labour but a broader understanding and respect for each other's time, abilities, and contributions. It's not merely about assigning tasks but about establishing a system that acknowledges each person's value to the household.

For example, one partner may be particularly adept at managing finances while the other excels at cooking. Acknowledging these strengths can result in a more efficient and harmonious home life where everyone feels valued and competent in their responsibilities. This mutual acknowledgment can also reduce the likelihood of resentment or tension arising from an unfair or imbalanced division of chores.

Moreover, the division of chores should not be a static arrangement but a flexible agreement that can adapt as circumstances change. Life events such as a new job, the arrival of a child, or a move to a different location can necessitate a reevaluation of household responsibilities. Periodic check-ins can be beneficial to ensure that both parties are satisfied with the arrangement and to make any adjustments as needed. In this way, determining who does what around the house becomes an ongoing dialogue, a dynamic aspect of relationship management rather than a one-time decision.

The chore list in a relationship is more than just a utilitarian division of tasks. It's a manifestation of the respect, understanding, and collaboration that are vital for a successful partnership. By approaching this aspect of domestic life thoughtfully and openly, couples can build a stronger, more equitable, and more fulfilling relationship.

Tools to Help Address the Past

Addressing past experiences and their impact on your current relationship is a multifaceted process that often requires an assortment of tools and strategies. Utilizing these resources can provide both

ADDRESSING ISSUES

partners with the insights and coping mechanisms necessary for dealing with complex emotional baggage. Here are some detailed tools and how they can be effectively employed:

Professional Help

Therapists, counsellors, psychologists, and other mental health professionals are trained to help people navigate the complexities of emotional issues, including those rooted in past experiences. Individual therapy can help one understand personal emotional triggers. In contrast, couples therapy can provide a safe space for both partners to discuss how past experiences may affect their relationship openly. Specialists in those areas can provide targeted treatments if there are specific issues like addiction or trauma.

Open Communication

Effective, open communication is the cornerstone of any strong relationship, especially when dealing with sensitive issues related to past experiences. This involves more than just talking; it's about creating an environment where both partners feel safe enough to express their deepest fears, concerns, and expectations. This can be facilitated through regular check-ins, setting aside time for deep conversations, and possibly using structured communication techniques like "I-statements" to prevent defensive reactions.

Support Groups

Joining a support group can provide a community of individuals facing similar challenges, thereby offering new perspectives and coping strategies that you may not have considered. Whether it's a group for divorcees, addiction recovery, or survivors of abuse, the shared experiences and advice can be invaluable. However, ensuring that the group's dynamics and guidelines are conducive to your healing process is crucial.

Journaling

Addressing Needs, Wants, & Desires

Writing down your thoughts, feelings, and observations can be a powerful tool for self-reflection and emotional processing. Journaling can help you identify patterns in your behaviour or thinking that may be rooted in past experiences. It can also serve as a tool for tracking emotional progress and changes in perspective over time.

Boundaries and limitations

Setting clear emotional and physical boundaries and limitations is essential when dealing with past issues. These boundaries help create a secure space where both partners can operate without fear of triggering past traumas or reigniting old conflicts. Articulated boundaries also offer a framework within which the relationship can grow, free from the shadows of past experiences.

Self-Care

Engaging in self-care activities can play a pivotal role in emotional well-being, which, in turn, affects relationship health. Exercise, mindfulness meditation, reading, or pursuing hobbies are not just ways to pass the time; they are avenues for personal growth and emotional rejuvenation. When you are in a better emotional state, you are better equipped to address past issues constructively.

Each tool and strategy offers a unique approach to dealing with the intricate emotional landscape that past experiences can create within a relationship. Employing a combination of these tools, customized to fit the specific challenges you and your partner face, can provide a comprehensive approach to addressing the past. It's an ongoing process that requires mutual effort, but the result is a stronger, more resilient relationship better equipped to face future challenges.

PARENTING *EACH* **OTHER**

In the intricate dance of a romantic relationship, partners bring their unique personalities, past experiences, and expectations to the table. These elements, rich in their individuality, contribute to the relationship's complexity and depth. However, they can also introduce specific dynamics that, if left unchecked, can become detrimental to the health of the relationship. One such complex dynamic is the tendency for one partner to "parent" the other. This dynamic can present itself in various forms and degrees, but it consistently raises questions about equality, autonomy, and the distribution of power within the relationship.

While some might argue that certain aspects of "parenting" behaviour—such as caring for your partner when they're sick or offering advice in difficult situations—are natural and even desirable in a romantic relationship, the critical difference lies in the balance and reciprocity of these actions. In a healthy relationship, both partners should feel capable of making decisions and managing their own lives, even sharing those lives with someone else. The shift from caring to "parenting" often involves one partner taking on excessive responsibility and control, leading to an imbalance that can compromise the partnership's integrity.

This chapter explores the multifaceted issue of "parenting" within relationships. We will explore the motivations behind this dynamic, its potential impact, and the strategies for addressing it effectively. The chapter will also examine closely related topics such as control and mutual respect, which often intersect with "parenting" behaviours. Understanding the concept of "parenting" in a relationship is not just an intellectual exercise but a practical tool that can help partners navigate one of the many complexities that come with sharing a life with someone else.

Examining this topic is especially crucial because the ramifications of a "parenting" dynamic can extend beyond the immediate relationship to affect other areas of life, including career choices, friendships, and even mental health. It can lead to a dependency where the "parented" partner may feel lost or incapable without the guidance of their significant other. On the flip side, the "parenting" partner may feel overwhelmed by the constant need to oversee another adult's life, which can lead to burnout and resentment.

So, as we unpack the complexities and nuances of this subject, our goal is to provide a comprehensive understanding that equips you with the knowledge and tools to identify and address any "parenting" tendencies within your relationship. This enriches your partnership and contributes to your personal growth and emotional well-being.

Parenting in a Relationship

The concept of "parenting" within the context of an adult romantic relationship refers to a dynamic where one partner assumes a role that resembles more of a parent than an equal partner. In essence, one person becomes the primary decision-maker, advisor, and even disciplinarian, treating the other partner as though they were less capable or less responsible. While the motivations behind this behaviour can vary, they often stem from a desire to care for, protect, or guide the other person. However well-intentioned this may be, it frequently results in an imbalance of power in the relationship that can lead to various negative consequences.

Such a dynamic can make the "parented" individual feel disempowered, less competent, and even resentful over time. Conversely, the "parenting" partner may become burdened by the added responsibility and feel more like a caretaker than an equal participant in the relationship. This imbalance can erode the foundation of mutual respect and equality, which is crucial for any healthy partnership. The "parenting" behaviour can manifest in various ways, including offering unsolicited advice, making unilateral decisions about plans or finances, and providing constant reminders or critiques about everyday tasks.

It's important to note that the "parenting" dynamic can be fluid, meaning that both partners may engage in this behaviour to varying degrees and in different contexts. Sometimes, this dynamic can be subtle and unintentional, making it even more challenging to identify and address. Regardless of its origins or intentions, the impact of a "parenting" dynamic on a relationship is generally detrimental and can hinder both partners' emotional growth and autonomy. Therefore, recognizing and addressing this pattern is crucial for the relationship's long-term health and the well-being of both individuals involved.

Avoid Parenting in the Relationship

Avoiding the parenting dynamic in a relationship is essential to maintaining a healthy balance of power and autonomy between partners. This balance is fundamental to ensuring that both individuals can fully participate in the relationship as equals. The first step to avoiding a parenting dynamic is recognizing its existence. Awareness is crucial, as many people unconsciously fall into the role of a parent or child, influenced by past experiences or societal norms. If either partner notices that a parenting dynamic is developing, it should be acknowledged and openly discussed.

Addressing Needs, Wants, & Desires

Open communication is critical to resolving this issue. Both partners should be able to express their concerns and feelings without fear of judgment. This open dialogue is not a one-time discussion but an ongoing process that evolves with the relationship. During these conversations, using "I" statements is essential to avoid blaming or accusing the other person. For example, instead of saying, "You always tell me what to do," you could say, "I feel like I'm being controlled when you tell me what to do all the time."

Sometimes, the person taking on the parental role believes they act in the other's best interest. While the intention might be caring or protective, the impact can be disempowering for the other partner. Hence, it's essential to consider not just the intent but also the effect of your actions on your partner.

It's also helpful to examine why the parenting dynamic is emerging. Sometimes, it stems from a lack of trust in the other person's capabilities or from one's own need for control. Understanding the root cause can help both partners work on underlying issues individually or as a couple. This could involve personal reflection, open dialogue, or professional guidance from a therapist or counsellor.

Moreover, both partners should focus on fostering an environment where decision-making is a collaborative process and each person's autonomy is respected. In practical terms, this could mean consulting each other on significant decisions that affect the relationship or the household rather than one person unilaterally making choices. It could also involve dividing responsibilities based on each person's strengths and preferences rather than assigning roles based on perceived capability or authority.

Avoiding a parenting dynamic in a relationship involves mutual respect, open communication, self-awareness, and a commitment to maintaining an equal partnership. It's an ongoing effort that requires both partners to be vigilant and willing to adjust their behaviour for a healthier, more balanced relationship.

PARENTING EACH OTHER

Controlling in a Relationship

Control within the context of a romantic relationship is a complex and multifaceted phenomenon that can manifest in various ways. At its core, control involves one partner exerting an inordinate amount of influence or authority over the other. This can range from subtle manipulations to overt commands and can affect multiple dimensions of the relationship, including emotional, psychological, and even physical aspects.

The expression of control can take many forms. It might be reflected in decision-making processes, where one partner unilaterally decides on matters that ideally involve mutual consent, such as financial planning or choosing social activities. It can also surface in behavioural expectations, dictating what is deemed acceptable or unacceptable behaviour for the other partner. For example, a controlling person might insist on knowing their partner's whereabouts at all times or may try to isolate them from friends and family.

The issue of control can even extend to more private spheres, such as personal beliefs, opinions, and emotions. In extreme cases, a controlling partner may employ tactics like gaslighting to manipulate the other into questioning their judgment and reality, thereby gaining emotional or psychological leverage over them.

Control is often a symptom of deeper issues within the relationship or the individual exerting the control. It may stem from insecurities, past traumas, or a lack of trust, leading to a toxic relationship environment if not addressed. Such behaviour undermines the foundation of mutual respect and equality that should characterize any healthy partnership.

It's essential to recognize that control is not the same as mutual influence, which is a natural and healthy part of any relationship. In a balanced partnership, both individuals have an equal say and consider each other's thoughts, feelings, and opinions when making decisions that affect the relationship. Control becomes problematic when this balance shifts and one person takes on a disproportionately influential role, negating the other's autonomy and voice.

Addressing control within a relationship often requires open communication and a commitment to change from the controlling partner. However, professional intervention may be necessary in severe cases where manipulative or abusive behaviours are present. Couples therapy or individual counselling can offer valuable insights and coping mechanisms for tackling control issues and restoring balance to the relationship.

Avoid Controlling in the Relationship

Avoiding control in a relationship is fundamentally about fostering a sense of equality and mutual respect between both partners. When control becomes a dominant factor in a relationship, it often leads to an imbalance of power, undermining the partnership's foundation. Control can manifest in various ways, such as dictating what your partner should wear, eat or whom they should associate with. It could extend to more subtle forms like undermining their decisions or questioning their judgments in a way that erodes their confidence.

To steer clear of controlling behaviour, the first step is self-awareness. Recognize the moments when you feel the urge to control your partner's actions or decisions and "bite your tongue." Ask yourself what underlying fears or insecurities prompt this need to exert authority. Is it a fear of loss, a need for security, or perhaps a lack of trust in your partner's capabilities? Identifying the root cause can be an enlightening experience, often requiring deep introspection or professional guidance through counselling or therapy.

Open dialogue plays a vital role in combating control. Frequent and honest communication can help both partners understand each other's needs, expectations, and apprehensions. If you find yourself wanting to control specific aspects of your partner's life, discuss it openly with them. Understand their perspective and explain yours without making it an authoritative directive. This dialogue should be two-way, where both partners feel heard and respected.

Active listening is another tool that can help in avoiding control. The urge to control often comes from not fully understanding your partner's point of view, leading to assumptions or judgments. By genuinely listening to what your partner is saying, you may find that the need to control diminishes. Listening can foster a greater understanding and, by extension, a more profound respect for each other's autonomy and individuality.

Another practical step to avoid control is to make decisions collaboratively. Whether it's something as simple as choosing a restaurant for dinner or as significant as deciding to relocate for a job, involving your partner in the decision-making process ensures that you both have equal say. This collaborative approach underscores the idea that you are in the relationship as equals and that one does not have authority over the other.

Furthermore, maintaining individuality is crucial in avoiding a controlling dynamic. Both partners should have the freedom to pursue their interests, friendships, and passions outside the relationship. Respecting this individual space can lead to a healthier, more balanced partnership where control is less likely to become an issue.

Avoiding control in a relationship involves a multifaceted approach that includes self-awareness, open communication, active listening, collaborative decision-making, and a deep-seated respect for each other's individuality and autonomy. It's a continuous effort that requires vigilance, empathy, and a willingness to adapt and grow individually and as a couple.

Stop Putting Each Other Down

Putting each other down in a relationship is a destructive behaviour that not only erodes the self-esteem of the recipient but also undermines the foundational trust and respect that sustain a healthy

Addressing Needs, Wants, & Desires

partnership. Such actions or comments often reflect deeper issues within the relationship or within the individual delivering them. It could be a manifestation of one's own insecurities, fears, or frustrations, projected onto the partner as a form of emotional release or even control.

To stop this cycle, the first step is awareness and acknowledgment. Both parties need to recognize that this behaviour is occurring and that it is harmful. This recognition often requires introspection, possibly even requiring the guidance of a therapist or counsellor to fully understand the underlying causes. It's crucial to be honest with oneself and each other about why this behaviour exists. Are you trying to exert control over your partner? Is it an expression of your insecurities or inadequacies? Or perhaps, is it a learned behaviour from past relationships or family dynamics?

Once the reasons are better understood, the next step is open communication between both partners. This is the time for heartfelt conversations, where each can express how the negative comments or actions have affected them emotionally and psychologically. This conversation should be a safe space, free from judgments or interruptions, where everyone feels heard and validated.

An apology is often necessary but should be genuine and accompanied by a commitment to change. Mere words are insufficient; actions must demonstrate the commitment to stop the harmful behaviour. This may involve setting up new communication guidelines, learning conflict resolution skills, or seeking couples therapy for more structured intervention.

Furthermore, it's essential to develop empathy towards each other. Try to understand your partner's point of view and feelings. Practicing empathy can often deter the impulse to put each other down because you become more sensitive to the impact of your words and actions. It fosters a kinder, more nurturing environment conducive to a healthy, respectful relationship.

Stopping the habit of putting each other down is a multi-faceted process that involves self-awareness, open communication, a genuine apology, and a commitment to change, often supported by professional guidance. By taking these steps, you work to rebuild the trust and respect that are so vital for a healthy and fulfilling relationship.

Addressing Issues and Problems

Addressing issues and problems without letting emotions overrun the conversation is a skill that often takes time and practice to develop. While emotions are integral to our human experience and can provide valuable insights into our needs and desires, they can also cloud judgment and impede effective communication. Emotional reactions can sometimes act as roadblocks, creating defensiveness or escalating conflicts rather than facilitating understanding and resolution.

One technique to maintain emotional equilibrium is to pause and take deep breaths before responding to a contentious point. This simple act can help you become more aware of your emotional state and allow you a moment to choose a more measured response. Another strategy is to take brief time-outs during heated discussions. Stepping away from the situation, even for just a few minutes, can provide both parties with the space to cool down and collect their thoughts, making the subsequent conversation more productive.

Writing down your thoughts can also be beneficial. This exercise forces you to articulate your feelings and concerns more clearly, which can help you understand them better and make it easier to communicate them to your partner. Sometimes, seeing your thoughts on paper can provide a fresh perspective on the issue, making it easier to approach the discussion more rationally.

Additionally, it may be helpful to establish specific "rules of engagement" for difficult conversations. For example, both parties could agree to avoid raising their voices, interrupting each other, or using accusatory language. Setting these guidelines in advance can

Addressing Needs, Wants, & Desires

provide a framework that encourages respectful and productive dialogue.

It's also worth mentioning that while the aim is to manage emotions during problem-solving discussions, this doesn't mean suppressing them. Emotions can offer valuable insights into the issues and should be acknowledged. The key is not to let them derail the conversation or prevent you from hearing your partner's perspective.

Practicing active listening can be incredibly beneficial in these situations. This means not just hearing the words your partner is saying but really trying to understand the meaning behind them. It involves asking clarifying questions and refraining from formulating your response while your partner is still speaking, allowing you to fully engage with their point of view.

By incorporating these strategies, couples can learn to address issues in a manner that is both emotionally sensitive and constructively rational. This balanced approach facilitates better understanding, fosters mutual respect, and ultimately contributes to a more harmonious relationship.

Separate Issues From Each Other

Separating issues from each other and joining strengths to problem-solve represents a mature and effective way to navigate challenges in a relationship. Instead of seeing problems as inherent traits or flaws in your partner, it's crucial to view them as external issues that both of you can work together to resolve. This approach shifts the focus from blame and accusation to collaborative problem-solving, which is far more conducive to a healthy relationship.

When a problem arises, it's easy to get wrapped up in the emotional intensity of the moment and start attributing the issue to your partner's character or behaviour. However, this often leads to defensiveness and conflict rather than resolution. By consciously choosing to separate the issue from the person, you create a space where both partners can discuss the problem without feeling personally attacked. This space becomes a platform for constructive dialogue, where the issue can be examined from various angles, and potential solutions can be explored.

Leveraging each other's strengths in the problem-solving process can make it more efficient and less contentious. Each person brings unique skills, experiences, and perspectives to the relationship, which can be invaluable resources when tackling challenges. For instance, if one partner is good at big-picture thinking while the other excels at details, these complementary skills can be combined to develop a comprehensive solution to a problem.

In practical terms, this might mean holding a "strategy session" where both partners can lay out their thoughts on the issue at hand. Each person can contribute ideas for potential solutions, drawing on their strengths. The key here is to listen to each other's contributions with an open mind and a focus on the ultimate goal of resolving the issue. During this discussion, it can be helpful to take notes, as this not only aids in remembering what has been said but also shows that you take the other's contributions seriously.

Sometimes, even after extensive discussion, a perfect solution that satisfies both parties may not be evident. Trying multiple solutions and assessing their effectiveness over time may be helpful in such cases. It's also important to be willing to revisit the issue and adjust the chosen solution as needed.

By adopting this collaborative approach to problem-solving, you and your partner can deal with challenges more effectively and with less emotional strife. This not only leads to better outcomes but also strengthens the relationship by fostering a sense of teamwork and mutual respect. This practice of separating issues from the people involved and combining strengths for problem-solving can be a powerful tool for maintaining a healthy, fulfilling relationship.

Addressing Needs, Wants, & Desires
Agree to Disagree

The concept of agreeing to disagree is essential in the context of a relationship, especially for issues that provoke strong opinions or emotional responses. This is not merely a phrase to be thrown around but a deliberate relationship strategy that signifies high maturity and respect between partners. It means that after discussing an issue, presenting arguments, and listening to each other's perspectives, both partners come to the realization that neither is going to change the other's mind. At this point, agreeing to disagree is a conscious decision to accept that having differing opinions on specific subjects is okay and that these differences do not necessarily have to be a point of contention or division.

When you agree to disagree, you acknowledge your partner's right to hold views different from your own without belittling them or questioning their intelligence or judgment. This action inherently involves a profound level of mutual respect. It means you value the relationship more than winning an argument or proving a point. It consists in letting go of the ego, which often wants to be correct at all costs, and instead choosing the path of emotional harmony.

This approach can be particularly useful for highly divisive issues or where compromise seems impossible. By agreeing to disagree, you can avoid getting caught in an endless loop of arguments that only serve to create tension and resentment. Importantly, this doesn't mean you ignore important issues or sweep them under the rug; instead, it's an acknowledgment that some issues might not have a resolution that satisfies both parties completely, and that's okay.

However, it's crucial to note that agreeing to disagree is not a one-size-fits-all solution. Finding common ground is often necessary for fundamental issues that affect the relationship's core, such as values, ethical beliefs, or plans for the future. But for less critical topics, agreeing to disagree can be a way to preserve the relationship's integrity while maintaining each partner's individuality.

Agreeing to disagree is valuable for maintaining a peaceful, respectful, and balanced relationship. It allows for individual opinions and beliefs within a collective partnership. It reinforces that a relationship involves two unique individuals who come together to enrich each other's lives rather than two people who must see eye-to-eye on every issue.

Tools to Avoid Parenting and Controlling

1. **Active Listening**: Pay full attention to your partner when discussing issues without interrupting or immediately offering solutions.
2. **Open Dialogue**: Keep the lines of communication open, allowing for honest discussion of feelings and concerns.
3. **Boundaries and Limitations**: Establishing clear boundaries can help maintain an equal power dynamic.
4. **Self-awareness**: Be conscious of your tendencies to control or be controlled and actively work to address them.
5. **Professional Help**: Counseling or therapy can provide further insights and coping mechanisms.

Navigating the pitfalls of parenting or controlling behaviour within a relationship is crucial for maintaining a healthy mutual respect and equality dynamic. This balance allows both partners to contribute their best selves to the partnership, enriching each other's lives and fostering a stronger, more harmonious relationship.

Addressing Needs, Wants, & Desires

PRACTICAL FERTILIZERS

Welcome to Week 9 of our guide, focused on what could be best described as "Practical Fertilizers." The metaphor of a relationship as a garden is an apt one. Just as a garden requires regular watering, the right balance of sun and shade, and protection from pests to flourish, a relationship also requires unique nourishment and care. You wouldn't expect a neglected garden to yield lush flowers or healthy vegetables. Similarly, an untended relationship is unlikely to bring about emotional satisfaction or personal growth for the parties involved.

The focus of this week is to delve into the practical aspects of nurturing your relationship. Just as fertilizers enrich the soil and promote plant growth, specific actions, behaviours, and mindsets can enhance the quality of your relationship. These strategies aim to deepen your emotional connection, heighten your physical intimacy, and strengthen the mutual respect and trust that are the bedrock of any successful partnership. We'll be exploring questions that may seem straightforward but are pivotal to the health of your relationship. How do you effectively communicate? How can you be more affectionate? What are the essentials that you absolutely can't compromise on?

Addressing Needs, Wants, & Desires

It's important to remember that every relationship is different, just as every garden has its unique soil composition, microclimate, and ecosystem. The "fertilizers" that work wonders in one relationship may not be as effective in another. Therefore, it's crucial to approach the advice and strategies presented in this chapter as a starting point. Feel free to adapt them to better suit the unique dynamics and needs of your relationship.

The act of focusing on these practical fertilizers is, in itself, an investment in your relationship. It signifies that you are both willing to put in the work to improve the quality of your partnership. This is a reassuring sign. Even the most substantial relationships can benefit from periodic maintenance. On the other hand, relationships going through rough patches may find that focusing on these practical aspects can help reset and reorient their priorities, paving the way for more profound emotional healing and connection.

In the following sections, we will explore these 'fertilizers' in detail. We will discuss methods to cultivate your relationship, grow love, and build trust, among other crucial topics. This chapter aims to equip you with a toolkit of practical strategies and insights; think of it as your gardening kit to help your relationship blossom. As you read through, you might find it beneficial to pause and discuss each section with your partner. After all, a garden grows best when tended by more than one pair of hands.

Cultivate Relationship

Cultivating a relationship is a complex endeavour likened to tending to a garden. It involves various interconnected actions, behaviours, and attitudes that contribute to the health and growth of the partnership. Just as a garden needs soil, water, sunlight, and regular attention to thrive, a relationship requires a fertile emotional environment sustained by multiple elements like open communication, mutual respect, and an ongoing investment of time and emotional energy.

PRACTICAL FERTILIZERS

When we speak of cultivation in this context, we're talking about active engagement. It's not enough to simply exist alongside another person; you have to actively work on understanding each other's needs, desires, and aspirations. This means having regular check-ins to discuss the relationship's state, planning and sharing experiences that bring you closer, and taking the time to express appreciation and love. It also involves negotiating conflicts and differences in a respectful manner and finding ways to compromise or meet in the middle for the benefit of both parties.

Moreover, relationship cultivation goes beyond just attending to the present moment. It's about planning for the future and working collaboratively to achieve shared goals, whether raising a family, buying a home, or simply navigating life's ups and downs together. When both partners are committed to the relationship's long-term health and work together to maintain it, they create a resilient partnership capable of withstanding challenges.

Cultivation also involves recognizing and addressing issues or unhealthy behaviours that could stunt the relationship's growth. Just like a gardener prunes away dead branches and pulls out weeds, couples need to be able to identify and rectify problems that could potentially harm the relationship in the long run. This could involve anything from correcting poor communication habits to seeking external help for more significant issues like trust or intimacy problems.

An important aspect of cultivation is adaptability. Relationships are not static; they evolve over time as both individuals grow and change. As a result, the methods of cultivation may need to be adapted to fit the changing landscape of the relationship. This might involve updating shared goals, renegotiating roles and responsibilities, or adopting new communication strategies to suit each phase of the relationship better.

Cultivating a relationship is an ongoing, multifaceted process that requires active participation from both partners. It involves love and affection, a significant emotional investment, open communication, mutual respect, and a willingness to adapt and grow together. By tending to these various elements, you create a robust, resilient relationship that can flourish over time.

Grow Love

Growing love within a relationship is a continual and evolving process that extends far beyond the initial stages of attraction and infatuation. While the early phases of a relationship often come with an intense feeling of passion, sustaining and growing love requires conscious effort, mutual respect, and a series of shared experiences that deepen the bond between two individuals. It is often a multifaceted endeavour involving various forms of intimacy—emotional, intellectual, and physical—that strengthen the relationship over time.

One fundamental way to grow love is through the cultivation of mutual respect. This involves recognizing and valuing each other's individuality, strengths, and weaknesses. Mutual respect creates a foundation upon which more complex emotional structures can be built, including trust and deep emotional connection. It is the soil in which love can take root and flourish.

Shared experiences are another critical element in growing love. Whether these are challenges you've overcome together, adventures you've shared, or simply quiet moments of connection, these experiences serve as building blocks in the narrative of your relationship. They create a shared history and a reservoir of memories that can be comforting and binding.

Emotional intimacy, which involves opening up and being vulnerable with each other, is another cornerstone. This emotional closeness allows you to understand your partner on a deeper level and fosters a sense of security and belonging. Emotional intimacy often leads to a more satisfying physical relationship, which in turn can serve

PRACTICAL FERTILIZERS

as a form of non-verbal communication that further deepens your emotional bond.

Expressing appreciation and gratitude towards your partner is also crucial in growing love. This can be done through verbal affirmations, acts of service, or any other "love language" that resonates with your partner. These acts serve as continual reminders of the love you share and reinforce the emotional connection between you.

Moreover, growth in love often involves a form of mutual evolution. As individuals grow and change, the relationship must adapt to accommodate these changes. This can involve renegotiating boundaries, adopting new shared goals, or finding new ways to support each other's individual pursuits. Open communication is vital in this aspect, as understanding how to navigate these changes can be complex and fraught with potential misunderstandings.

Growing love in a relationship is not a passive process that occurs spontaneously; it's an active endeavour that requires attention, effort, and a willingness to adapt and evolve together. By focusing on mutual respect, shared experiences, emotional intimacy, and open communication, couples can foster a deep, enduring love that stands the test of time.

Be Affectionate

Being affectionate in a relationship is a multifaceted endeavour that extends beyond simple physical gestures. While physical touch—such as hugs, kisses, cuddling and bantering—certainly plays a significant role in expressing affection, there are numerous other ways to show love and care for your partner. The expression of affection can manifest in verbal affirmations, where words of love, compliments, and expressions of gratitude can profoundly impact your partner's emotional well-being. Saying "I love you," paying a genuine compliment, or thanking your partner for something they've done can serve as powerful affirmations of your feelings.

Addressing Needs, Wants, & Desires

Moreover, acts of service can also be a form of affection. These are actions you take to make your partner's life easier, ranging from small daily tasks like making coffee in the morning to more considerable efforts like planning a surprise weekend getaway. These acts show thoughtfulness and consideration, signalling that you value your partner's comfort and happiness.

Quality time is another crucial element in showing affection. Spending time together, free from distractions, allows for deeper emotional connections to form. Whether it's a quiet dinner, a walk in the park, or simply sitting together in comfortable silence, quality time allows couples to connect more intimately.

Though not necessary for everyone, gift-giving can also be a way to show affection. Thoughtful gifts that show you know and understand your partner can be deeply touching. However, the emphasis here is on the thoughtfulness behind the gift rather than its monetary value. Even simple, inexpensive gifts can be powerful expressions of affection if they demonstrate a deep understanding of your partner's likes and needs.

The key to compelling affection lies in understanding how your partner receives love and tailoring your actions accordingly. Some people may value physical touch more highly, while others may prefer verbal affirmations or acts of service. Open communication about how each of you perceives and receives affection can help both partners feel more loved and valued in the relationship.

Therefore, being affectionate isn't limited to any one action or gesture; it's a composite of various behaviours and expressions that demonstrate your love and appreciation. By paying attention to your partner's preferences and consciously showing affection in a way that resonates with them, you enrich the emotional fabric of your relationship, making it more fulfilling for both parties involved.

PRACTICAL FERTILIZERS

Necessary and Mandatory

In any relationship, there are certain elements that are not just beneficial but are fundamentally necessary for the relationship's sustainability and growth. These mandatory elements serve as the underpinnings of a healthy, functioning partnership and are often non-negotiable for long-term success. Communication, trust, and mutual respect are the most crucial of these.

Communication is indispensable because it is through open and honest dialogue that couples are able to express their needs, share their feelings, resolve conflicts, and make collaborative decisions. Misunderstandings can quickly occur without effective communication, leading to unnecessary conflicts and emotional distance. Open communication channels enable couples to discuss everything from daily logistics to deep emotional needs, fostering an environment where both individuals feel heard and understood.

Trust serves as the cornerstone upon which all other aspects of the relationship are built. Without trust, elements like vulnerability, emotional intimacy, and essential reliability become jeopardized. Trust is earned through consistent honesty, integrity, and emotional availability. It's fortified each time a promise is kept, support is provided in moments of need, and honesty prevails over deceit. Losing trust can have a domino effect, destabilizing other areas of the relationship making its maintenance a mandatory focus for both parties.

Mutual respect is another essential factor, often interlinked with trust and communication. Respect in a relationship manifests as valuing each other's opinions, listening without interrupting, giving each other additional personal space, and showing consideration in actions and words. It also means acknowledging each other's individuality and appreciating each person's unique qualities in the relationship. Without mutual respect, there's a risk of the relationship devolving into a power struggle, where one individual's needs and opinions overshadow the other's, creating an imbalanced and unhealthy dynamic.

Addressing Needs, Wants, & Desires

Additional components often considered necessary include emotional and physical safety, shared values, and aligned life goals. Emotional and physical safety ensures that each partner feels secure in expressing themselves and their physical interactions. Shared values and aligned life goals provide a common direction for the relationship, offering a framework within which both partners can grow individually and as a couple.

While each relationship is unique and may have its requirements for success, certain foundational elements are universally acknowledged as essential. These serve as the building blocks for a stable, fulfilling partnership, and their presence—or absence—can often predict the long-term viability of the relationship.

Affection and Sex

Affection and sex hold pivotal roles in a romantic relationship as integral conduits for emotional and physical intimacy. Affection is a broad term that encompasses various forms of tender behaviour, including but not limited to verbal affirmations, touching, hugging, and kissing. These acts of affection function as emotional touchpoints that strengthen the bond between partners, reinforcing a sense of closeness, security, and belonging. They offer a way to express love and appreciation in a tangible manner, affirming the relationship's emotional health and the partners' mutual respect.

Sexual intimacy, on the other hand, goes beyond affection to include a more explicit form of physical closeness. It serves as a unique form of communication, allowing partners to express their love, desire, and emotional connection in a way that words often can't capture. But it's not just about the physical act but also about the emotional and psychological components accompanying it. A healthy sexual relationship is one in which both partners feel emotionally safe, physically satisfied, and connected. This involves mutual consent, respect for each other's boundaries, and open communication about desires and preferences.

PRACTICAL FERTILIZERS

Sex is a craving most individuals desire. It may appear that it is most common among men; however, the time has changed where women desire sex. Considering the fact that sex and sexual pleasure are a multibillion-dollar industry around the world, couples need to tap into making it enjoyable and satisfying to avoid the need to be fulfilled elsewhere. Relationship fails due to lack of sex or boring sex. Lack of sex can lead to onanism, self-satisfying sex, pornography, exploitation, meeting escorts, and other means to satisfy the desire for sex.

Some individuals desire same-sex pleasure as they are not satisfied by their partner; some prefer open relationships, monogamous relationships, group sex and more. Healthy sex should be maintained in the relationship. One partner may not have a strong sex drive, may not feel sexually attractive or does feel they can satisfy their partner, but that should not become an issue in the relationship. Couples must learn to compromise and complement each other to avoid infidelity and other issues that may arise due to a lack of healthy sex.

Notably, the absence or lack of affection and sex can be symptomatic of underlying issues in the relationship, such as emotional distance, unresolved conflicts, or even external stressors like work or health problems. Thus, maintaining a healthy level of both affection and sexual intimacy can serve as a barometer for the relationship's overall well-being.

Both affection and sex are interrelated and often influence each other. A relationship rich in affection often finds that this emotional closeness enhances the quality of the sexual relationship. Conversely, a fulfilling sexual relationship can boost emotional intimacy, creating a positive feedback loop that benefits the entire relationship.

In short, affection and sex are important because they foster emotional and physical intimacy, serving as vital elements in the complex emotional ecosystem of a romantic relationship. They provide avenues for expressing love, building trust, and maintaining a deep emotional connection, all of which are crucial for both partners' long-term health and happiness. To avoid infidelity, it is essential to have a healthy sex life.

Sex and Intimacy

The significance of sex and intimacy in a romantic relationship cannot be overstated. These two components serve multiple critical functions beyond physical pleasure or procreation. On a foundational level, sex and intimacy act as essential means of communication between partners, often expressing complex emotions, desires, and levels of trust that might be difficult to articulate through words alone.

Sexual intimacy contributes to the emotional fabric of a relationship in several ways. First, it fosters a unique form of closeness that generally isn't shared with anyone else, strengthening the romantic partnership's exclusivity and specialness. This unique form of closeness can generate a sense of security and emotional safety, which in turn promotes more open communication and vulnerability in other areas of the relationship.

Moreover, a fulfilling sexual relationship can be an emotional buffer during challenging times. The endorphins and oxytocin released during sexual activities are natural mood lifters and stress reducers. They also facilitate bonding, enhancing partners' emotional resilience when navigating difficulties either within or outside the relationship. Conversely, lack of sexual intimacy can exacerbate feelings of isolation, disconnection, or resentment, potentially leading to a downward spiral of relationship quality.

Sexual intimacy is also closely linked to self-esteem and body image. A satisfying sex life can boost self-confidence, which has a ripple effect on other areas of life, including career and social interactions. When both partners feel desirable and desired, it can create a positive feedback loop of mutual appreciation and affection.

It's important to note that healthy sexual intimacy is built on mutual consent, respect for each other's boundaries, and open

PRACTICAL FERTILIZERS

communication about desires and comfort levels. It's a two-way street that requires ongoing effort from both parties. Therefore, the absence of coercion, guilt-tripping, or emotional manipulation is crucial for sustaining a healthy sexual relationship. Both partners should feel free to express their sexual needs and boundaries without fear of judgment or retaliation.

Sex and intimacy hold a multifaceted role in romantic relationships, influencing emotional well-being, mutual trust, and even individual self-esteem. Their importance extends far beyond the act itself, serving as a barometer for the overall health and happiness of the relationship. Hence, investing in a satisfying and respectful sexual relationship is not just a matter of physical gratification but also an essential component in building and maintaining a strong, enduring partnership.

Healthy sex and intimacy are complex constructs that go beyond mere physical acts to include a range of emotional, psychological, and even spiritual elements. In a healthy sexual relationship, both partners experience a sense of mutual consent, which means that each person is actively and willingly participating. This consent is ongoing and can be revoked at any time, making continuous communication vital for maintaining a healthy sexual atmosphere.

Open communication is another critical aspect of healthy sex and intimacy. Both partners should feel free to express their desires, preferences, and boundaries without fear of judgment, ridicule, or coercion. This openness allows for a sexually fulfilling experience that respects each person's individuality and autonomy. It's not just about speaking but also about listening. Active listening skills can help you understand and respond to your partner's needs effectively, enhancing the sexual experience for both.

Emotional and physical safety are also foundational to healthy sex and intimacy. This safety encompasses not just the absence of harm but also the presence of comfort and trust. Emotional safety can manifest as feeling secure enough to be vulnerable with your partner. In contrast, physical safety often involves mutual respect for boundaries and may include protection to prevent unwanted pregnancies or sexually transmitted infections.

Additionally, healthy sex and intimacy are often enriched by a strong emotional connection between partners. While it's possible to have physical intimacy without emotional intimacy, the depth and fulfillment often increase when both are present. Emotional intimacy can act as a powerful form of communication, where actions express sentiments that words may fail to capture.

Healthy sex and intimacy in a relationship involve a complex interplay of mutual consent, open communication, emotional and physical safety, and, often, a solid emotional connection. Each of these elements contributes to a more fulfilling and respectful sexual relationship, making it a crucial aspect of the overall health and well-being of the partnership.

Effective Communication

Effective communication is often cited as the cornerstone of a successful relationship, and for good reason. It's the mechanism through which we express our needs, desires, frustrations, and affections. However, effective communication is not just about speaking clearly; it's a two-way street that involves articulating your thoughts and actively listening to your partner.

In the realm of effective communication, the importance of active listening cannot be overstated. Active listening is about hearing the spoken words and grasping the underlying feelings, intentions, and meanings. This involves not just listening with your ears but also with your eyes and heart. Notice your partner's body language, tone of voice, and any emotional cues hidden beneath the surface. Give them your full attention without formulating your response while they are still speaking, as this can detract from truly understanding what is being said.

PRACTICAL FERTILIZERS

Equally crucial is the ability to express yourself clearly, honestly, and respectfully. Transparency is critical; hiding your true feelings or thoughts can lead to misunderstandings and ultimately erode trust. At the same time, the way you convey these feelings matters. Speaking from a place of love and respect is essential, avoiding blame or accusations, which can put your partner on the defensive and hinder constructive dialogue. The objective is not to win an argument but to resolve issues collaboratively, reaching a mutual understanding or compromise.

Emotional intelligence plays a significant role in effective communication within a relationship. The ability to recognize, understand, and manage your own emotions and be aware of your partner's emotional state can make conversations more productive and less prone to escalating into conflicts. If you sense that emotions are running high, stepping back and cooling down might be beneficial before continuing the conversation.

Timing and setting are also crucial factors. Choose an appropriate time and place for meaningful conversations, free from distractions or external pressures. Sometimes, the most effective communication occurs when both parties are relaxed and comfortable, such as during a quiet dinner at home or a leisurely walk together.

Effective communication is a multifaceted skill that goes beyond mere verbal exchange. It involves active listening, emotional intelligence, transparent and respectful expression, and situational awareness. Mastering these elements can significantly enhance the quality of interactions with your partner, leading to a deeper, more fulfilling relationship. The key is to learn how to ride on each other's conversation and create a flow. It's a more organic and natural way of carrying on a never-ending conversation.

Addressing Needs, Wants, & Desires
Ride Conversations as a Speaker and Listener

The concept of riding conversations as both a speaker and listener involves a nuanced understanding of communication dynamics in a relationship. As a speaker, your role extends beyond merely conveying information. You're tasked with sharing your thoughts, feelings, and perspectives in a manner that is clear and considerate of your partner's emotional state and viewpoints. This requires a level of emotional intelligence to gauge the appropriate tone, timing, and phrasing of what you need to communicate. It's not just about what you say but how you say it. Framing your words in a way that invites dialogue rather than shutting it down is critical. For instance, using "I" statements like "I feel" or "I think" can make the conversation less accusatory and more open to mutual understanding.

As a listener, your role is equally complex and vital. Active listening goes beyond simply hearing the words that are spoken; it involves a deep engagement with the speaker, an attempt to understand not just the words but the emotions and intentions behind them. It means providing feedback, asking clarifying questions, and sometimes, offering validation. This form of listening creates a safe space for the speaker to express themselves fully, knowing they are genuinely heard and valued.

A balanced conversation, therefore, involves fluidly transitioning between the roles of speaker and listener. It's a dynamic dance where both partners contribute to the rhythm and flow of the dialogue. This balancing act is essential for meaningful, effective communication. Both parties should leave the conversation feeling heard, understood, and valued. Each should have the opportunity to speak their truth and listen to the other's, leading to a deeper mutual understanding that can strengthen the relationship.

Moreover, this dynamic isn't static; it evolves as the relationship grows and individuals change. As such, revisiting and reassessing your communication styles periodically is essential. External events, personal growth, or even mood can sometimes affect how well you perform as a speaker and listener. Being aware of these shifts and willing to adapt is crucial for maintaining a healthy communication dynamic in the relationship.

Building Trust

Building trust within a relationship is a complex, ongoing process involving many factors and behaviours. At its core, trust is the belief or confidence that one's partner will act in beneficial, honest, and considerate ways. This belief is nurtured not just by grand gestures or promises but also through everyday interactions and shared experiences. Trust is often built incrementally, accumulating over time as each partner proves reliable, transparent, and emotionally available.

Consistency is crucial when it comes to building trust. This means being reliable in your actions and reactions so your partner knows what to expect. Whether it's being punctual for dates or following through on promises, consistent behaviour demonstrates that you are a person of your word, which fosters trust.

Open and honest communication is another cornerstone in establishing trust. This involves more than just telling the truth; it also means being willing to discuss complex topics, admit when you're wrong, and share your feelings openly. When both partners are committed to transparent communication, it eliminates much of the guesswork and insecurity that can erode trust.

Emotional availability is also crucial. This means being there for your partner during emotional need, offering support, understanding, and empathy. It's about being emotionally present in the relationship and willing to share your vulnerabilities while respecting those of your partner. Emotional safety, where each person feels they can be their authentic selves without fear of judgment or rejection, is often a result of established trust.

Addressing Needs, Wants, & Desires

It's worth noting that trust is fragile and can be damaged more quickly than it is built. Acts of betrayal, such as lying or cheating, can quickly erode the trust that has been established, often requiring considerable time and effort to rebuild. In some cases, trust may be irreparably damaged, leading to the end of the relationship. Therefore, maintaining trust requires ongoing vigilance and commitment from both parties.

Moreover, trust is reciprocal. Both partners need to engage in behaviours that build trust and feel trust in the other for a balanced, healthy relationship to exist. It's a mutual investment that pays dividends in the form of a more secure, harmonious relationship. Trust also acts as a buffer during conflict, providing a stable foundation to resolve issues and navigate challenges.

Trust is a multifaceted, delicate aspect of relationships built through consistent, honest, and emotionally available behaviour. It serves as the foundational glue that holds a relationship together, and its presence or absence can profoundly impact the relationship's health and longevity.

Love Languages

The concept of "love languages" was popularized by Dr. Gary Chapman in his book "The Five Love Languages," where he outlines five primary ways people express and receive love. These are Words of Affirmation, Acts of Service, Receiving Gifts, Quality Time, and Physical Touch. Understanding love languages is crucial for enhancing emotional intimacy and connection in a relationship because it helps you recognize how your partner naturally expresses love and what makes them feel most loved.

For example, suppose one partner's primary love language is Words of Affirmation. In that case, they will deeply appreciate verbal expressions of love and affirmation, such as compliments, words of encouragement, and expressions of gratitude. On the other hand, if

PRACTICAL FERTILIZERS

another partner's primary love language is Acts of Service, they will feel most loved when their partner performs kind gestures, like taking care of a chore they dislike or preparing a meal for them.

Recognizing these different modes of expressing and receiving love can lead to more satisfying emotional exchanges. It can reduce misunderstandings and feelings of neglect or unappreciation that may arise when partners are not attuned to each other's primary love languages. For instance, a partner who primarily expresses love through Acts of Service might feel unappreciated if their gestures are not met with the enthusiasm they expect, especially if their partner's primary love language is Quality Time. They would rather spend meaningful moments together.

Growing the love languages in a relationship involves a two-fold approach. First, each partner should strive to understand their primary and secondary love languages, often achievable through self-reflection, discussions, or even taking quizzes designed to identify one's love language. Second, there should be an active effort to understand the partner's love languages and to express love in ways that resonate with them.

This may sometimes require stepping out of one's comfort zone. For instance, if you're not naturally inclined to give verbal affirmations but your partner's primary love language is Words of Affirmation, making a conscious effort to express love in this way can significantly enhance the emotional quality of the relationship. In essence, understanding and growing the love languages in a relationship is like learning a new dialect of a language—you're expanding your ability to communicate more effectively with your partner, which, in turn, enriches the emotional depth and connection in your relationship.

Growing the love languages involves understanding your primary love languages and those of your partner and consciously expressing love in a way that resonates with both. It may require

Addressing Needs, Wants, & Desires

stepping out of your comfort zone to effectively meet your partner's emotional needs.

Relationship Fertilizers

The term "relationship fertilizers" serves as a metaphor to describe the various actions, behaviours, or practices that positively contribute to a relationship's growth and stability, much like how fertilizer aids in the growth of plants. These fertilizers can take many forms and are deeply individualized based on the unique dynamics of each relationship. For some couples, a relationship fertilizer could be regular date nights that help rekindle romance and allow for quality time away from the hustle and bustle of daily life. For others, it might be leaving sweet notes for each other or making breakfast in bed.

Some fertilizers focus on emotional and psychological well-being. Heartfelt conversations where both partners can express their feelings, dreams, and fears can be a potent fertilizer. Acts of service, like taking care of a partner when they're ill or handling chores they dislike, can also contribute positively to relationship health. These actions show a level of care and consideration that reinforces the bond between partners.

Additionally, relationship fertilizers can also be more planned or structured. Some couples find that attending workshops, reading relationship-focused literature, or even engaging in couples therapy can serve as valuable fertilizers that bring new perspectives and tools into the relationship.

It's also worth noting that what serves as a fertilizer at one stage in a relationship might change as the relationship matures. Early on, exciting adventures and deep conversations might serve to deepen the connection. Later, shared responsibilities, mutual support during challenging times, or even the simple act of consistently showing up might take on greater significance.

PRACTICAL FERTILIZERS

One of the most extraordinary forms of fertilizer is using the dung from past flaws, mistakes, regrets, wrongdoing, and wrong choices. Instead of holding the past against each other, we need to use it to fertilize the future to avoid making the same mistakes twice.

Importantly, these fertilizers aren't just one-off actions but should be consistently applied over time. Just as a plant needs regular watering and nourishment, so does a relationship that requires ongoing positive actions to keep it healthy, vibrant, and growing. The consistent application of these positive actions or relationship fertilizers can play a crucial role in the long-term health and happiness of the partnership.

Bathe Relationships with Positive Fertilizers

The concept of "bathing relationships with positive fertilizers" expands on the idea of enriching your relationship through specific actions, behaviours, or practices that contribute to its growth and health. This involves identifying these "fertilizers" and consistently applying them in your daily interactions and overall approach to the relationship. The term "bathing" suggests a thorough, immersive experience, implying that these positive actions should not be sparse or occasional but should pervade the relationship continuously and sustainably.

For example, if one of the identified "fertilizers" in your relationship is quality time, then "bathing" the relationship in this positive action would mean deliberately carving out time from your busy schedules to focus solely on each other. This could be a weekly date night, a monthly weekend getaway, or even a few undistracted hours at home. The key is to make this a regular practice, not just a one-time event. Consistency is crucial here; the frequent application of these "fertilizers" leads to sustained relationship growth.

Similarly, if open communication is another identified "fertilizer," then "bathing" your relationship would foster an environment where both partners feel safe and encouraged to express their thoughts, feelings, and concerns openly. This could involve

Addressing Needs, Wants, & Desires

scheduled weekly check-ins to discuss the state of the relationship, or it could be a commitment to bring up issues as they arise rather than letting them fester.

If acts of service are a significant "fertilizer" for your relationship, then incorporating this into your daily life can make a meaningful impact. It could be as simple as making coffee for your partner in the morning or as involved as planning a surprise weekend trip to relieve stress. The aim is to regularly perform these acts of service to show your appreciation and love.

Regularly applying these "fertilizers" is like bathing the relationship in a nurturing solution that promotes health, resilience, and growth. Just as a bath cleanses and refreshes the body, consistently applying these positive actions cleanses the relationship of negativity, stagnation, or routine, infusing it with renewed energy and vitality. This consistent application helps ensure the relationship survives and thrives, becoming more robust, fulfilling, and harmonious.

Tools to Help Fertilize the Relationship

1. **Scheduled Check-ins**: Regular conversations to discuss the state of the relationship and any areas for improvement.
2. **Shared Activities**: Engaging in activities that both partners enjoy can strengthen the bond.
3. **Relationship Books and Workshops**: Sometimes, external resources can provide new insights or techniques for improving the relationship.
4. **Counselling or Therapy**: Professional help can offer targeted ways to improve relationship dynamics.

Relationships, like any living thing, require constant care and nourishment. By actively engaging in practices fostering growth and unity, you can help ensure a more vibrant, fulfilling partnership for both parties.

KISSING *BREAKUPS* GOODBYE

In the intricate dance of human relationships, the possibility of parting ways often looms as a shadow, subtly influencing choices, behaviours, and even the intensity of love itself. Whether you're navigating the exhilarating highs of a new relationship or the comfortable familiarity of a long-term partnership, the threat of a breakup can serve as both a cautionary tale and a catalyst for growth. It's a topic most couples would rather not dwell on, but addressing it head-on can provide invaluable insights that fortify your relationship against the trials it will inevitably face. In that sense, learning to "kiss breakups goodbye" is not just about avoiding an unpleasant outcome; it's about enriching your relationship to withstand the complexities and challenges of shared life experiences.

The title of this chapter may evoke a sense of finality as if there were a foolproof formula to prevent all breakups. But let's be clear: there are no guarantees in love or life. Relationships end for a myriad of reasons—some sudden and unforeseeable, others gradual and almost predictable. However, the focus here is not on creating an invincible romantic union but on cultivating a relationship robust enough to weather both internal and external storms. When both partners actively invest in strengthening their bond, they increase their resilience against potential breakups and enhance the overall quality of their relationship.

As we navigate through the various elements that serve as the "glue" in a stable, loving relationship, you'll notice that they often intertwine, reinforcing the others. From treating each other with dignity and respect, which lays the foundation for all interactions, to understanding the value of grooming and physical appearance as an external manifestation of internal love and respect, each component contributes to a holistic view of what makes a relationship endure. We'll explore why emotional and physical well-being is not individual pursuits but collective goals that significantly impact the relationship's health. We'll delve into the often overlooked but incredibly crucial aspect of building a shared culture, a mutual framework that provides common ground and a shared sky.

Beyond the physical and emotional realms, we will also examine relationships' intellectual and spiritual dimensions. How do you maintain the spark that fueled your initial attraction? What's the role of shared values and beliefs in sustaining a long-term partnership? How do you negotiate the balance between individual freedom and collective responsibility? These questions may not have easy answers. Still, they offer fertile ground for reflection and discussion, critical ingredients in the recipe for a lasting relationship.

So, as we embark on this exploration, remember that the objective is not merely to avoid the pain of separation but to enrich the joy of togetherness. It's not just about averting the end but about enhancing the journey, ensuring that each step is taken with love, respect, and a deep understanding of its significance in the larger narrative of your shared lives. Let's delve into the practical strategies and thoughtful insights that can help you and your partner kiss breakups goodbye, not out of fear of being alone but out of the desire to cultivate a love that endures.

Dignity and Respect

Treating each other with dignity and respect is not just a social nicety or a superficial aspect of a relationship; it's a fundamental cornerstone that impacts the partnership's overall quality, longevity, and health. Dignity refers to each individual's inherent value and worth, while respect is the active recognition and treatment of this worth in daily interactions. When you treat your partner with dignity, you acknowledge their inherent value as a person, separate from any conditional factors like status, achievements, or even the ebbs and flows of the relationship itself.

Respect, on the other hand, is the actionable aspect of dignity. It manifests in how you communicate with your partner, your consideration for their feelings and opinions, and the space you give them to be themselves. It means listening actively when they speak, honouring their choices and decisions, and interacting in a way that uplifts rather than diminishes. Respect also extends to the way conflicts are managed in the relationship. Even in heated moments of disagreement, maintaining a level of respect can prevent conversations from devolving into destructive patterns of communication, such as name-calling, contempt, or stonewalling.

Several vital outcomes occur when both partners engage in a mutual exchange of dignity and respect. First, it creates a safe emotional space where each individual can be vulnerable, essential for intimacy and deep emotional connection. Second, it establishes a level playing field, where the relationship becomes a partnership of equals rather than a hierarchy. This balance is crucial for empowering both parties to contribute fully to the relationship, secure in the knowledge that their input is valued and respected. Third, it sets up a positive feedback loop of behaviour; respect begets respect, creating a conducive environment for each partner to grow and thrive, individually and within the context of the relationship.

Moreover, a relationship grounded in dignity and respect is more resilient in facing challenges. Whether dealing with external pressures like work stress, family issues, or internal relationship hurdles like disagreements or emotional distance, foundational respect and dignity serve as a robust emotional cushion. This cushion can mitigate the impact of these stressors, often providing the couple with the emotional resources needed to navigate through them successfully.

Treating each other with dignity and respect is ethical and practical. It serves as the underpinning for many different healthy relationship dynamics, including effective communication, emotional intimacy, and resilience in the face of adversity. Thus, it's an indispensable element for any successful, long-lasting relationship.

Falling in Love, Dating and Having Fun

The process of falling in love is a multifaceted emotional experience often marked by a heightened sense of connection, attraction, and intrigue toward another person. During this phase, dating and engaging in fun activities together serve as fundamental building blocks for the relationship. These shared experiences offer opportunities for both partners to learn more about each other's personalities, interests, values, and quirks. Whether a simple dinner at a local restaurant or a more adventurous outing like hiking, these activities create a platform for mutual exploration and discovery.

But beyond just learning about each other, dating and having fun serve another vital role: they create a reservoir of positive memories and emotions that can act as a buffer during challenging times in the relationship. When conflicts arise or when the relationship undergoes stress, these positive memories serve as touchstones that remind each partner why they fell in love in the first place. They can help rekindle passion, reaffirm commitment, and inspire efforts to resolve whatever issues may be at hand.

Furthermore, engaging in fun activities fosters a sense of partnership and shared accomplishment. Successfully planning and executing a fun day or an exciting date night can boost feelings of teamwork and mutual competence. This strengthens the emotional bonds between partners and instills a sense of shared responsibility for the relationship's well-being.

The fun and excitement of dating do not just pertain to the early phases of a relationship; they should be sustained throughout its duration. Keeping that initial spark alive through ongoing dates and shared experiences is a way to invest in the relationship's emotional health continually. This continued investment can prevent feelings of stagnation or complacency, often precursors to more significant relationship issues.

In essence, the concepts of falling in love, including dating and having fun, are not just the initial stages of a relationship but are integral components that nourish and sustain it over the long term. These activities lay the groundwork for deeper emotional intimacy, foster a sense of mutual enjoyment and achievement, and create a pool of positive experiences that can help buoy the relationship through its inevitable ups and downs.

"First Love Syndrome"

The term "First Love Syndrome" captures the heady mix of excitement, novelty, and emotional intensity that often characterizes the initial stages of romantic relationships. This phase is marked by a heightened sense of wonder and idealization, where every interaction feels significant, and the emotional and physical connections are electrifying. During this period, couples are highly attentive to each other, quick to express affection and appreciation and deeply invested in mutual happiness.

While it's natural for this initial intensity to wane over time as the relationship matures and life's realities set in, maintaining aspects of this "First Love Syndrome" can offer numerous benefits for long-term relationship health. The sense of excitement and wonder can serve as a potent antidote to the monotony or routine that often creeps into long-term partnerships. It constantly reminds you of the emotional and physical chemistry that initially drew you to your partner, reinforcing the unique qualities that make your relationship special.

Moreover, this continual rekindling of early-stage affection and attention can help couples navigate the challenges and stresses that inevitably arise in any long-term commitment. When faced with obstacles, whether financial difficulties, health issues, or conflicts of any nature, the memory and ongoing experience of that initial "First Love" can serve as a strong motivational force. It encourages both partners to resolve issues collaboratively and to treat each other with kindness and respect, even during trying times.

By actively maintaining elements of your "First Love Syndrome," such as regular expressions of affection, spontaneous acts of kindness, or even the simple act of looking at your partner through the same rose-coloured glasses you wore when you first fell in love, you can inject a sense of enduring passion and excitement into your relationship. This not only enhances the quality of the relationship but also fortifies it against the various challenges you will face as a couple, making it more resilient and fulfilling for both parties involved.

In essence, keeping the "First Love Syndrome" alive in a long-term relationship isn't about denying the realities and complexities of love's mature stages. Instead, it's about infusing the mature, enduring aspects of your love with the joy, wonder, and idealism that characterized its beginning. This balanced approach ensures that the relationship remains a source of comfort and excitement, enhancing its longevity and the happiness of both individuals involved.

Best, Better, Bonus

The notion of "producing our best" in a relationship encapsulates the idea that each partner should bring their highest quality of self into the partnership emotionally and practically. This means continually striving for personal growth and self-improvement to enrich your life and your relationship. In a practical sense, bringing your best self into a relationship involves maintaining good communication skills, cultivating emotional intelligence, and nurturing an empathetic understanding of your partner's needs and feelings.

This concept goes beyond mere appearances or superficial traits; it's about maintaining a level of emotional maturity and stability that contributes positively to the relationship. It also involves nurturing qualities like patience, understanding, and kindness, which play a crucial role in any successful partnership. When you are committed to being your best self, you are more likely to address issues constructively rather than destructively, to listen with the intent to understand rather than to reply, and to approach challenges as opportunities for mutual growth.

Another critical aspect of producing your best in a relationship involves remaining engaged and active in the partnership. Complacency can be a significant relationship killer. When both parties continually invest effort into maintaining and improving their relationship, it fosters a positive environment where both individuals can flourish. Active engagement can take many forms, from planning regular date nights to keep the spark alive to actively working through conflicts and challenges rather than sweeping them under the rug.

It's also worth noting that bringing your best self into a relationship is not a one-time effort but a continuous process. People change, circumstances evolve, and the relationship itself will go through various phases. Your "best" today might not be your "best" five years from now. As such, this requires a willingness to adapt and grow as individuals and as a couple.

Producing your best in a relationship is an ongoing commitment involving emotional maturity and active engagement. It's about providing a version of yourself that enhances the quality of the relationship, meets your partner's emotional needs, and creates a supportive environment conducive to mutual growth and happiness. This commitment to excellence in the relationship often protects against many common issues couples face, laying the groundwork for a long-lasting, fulfilling partnership.

Addressing Needs, Wants, & Desires

After maturing and producing your best, you can take the relationship to another level, which is better than best. You explore every option as to what can be done to take the relationship to the next level to avoid boredom, complacency, and lack of interest. Taking the relationship from " best to better," your mind should focus on what you must do to keep the first love in the relationship. You see your best as the baseline of your relationship, and "better" is another level that is better than best.

After maturing from "best to better," you can take the relationship to the next level called "bonus." The "bonus" level creates expectancy in the relationship. It is when you do things for your partner that they would never expect. It's like a bonus cheque you received from your job that you never saw coming.

Take your relationships from best to better to bonus!

Our Physical and Mental Health

The importance of taking care of your physical and mental health in a relationship cannot be overstated, as well-being in these areas directly impacts the relationship's overall quality. When you're physically healthy, you're more likely to engage in activities together, experience less stress, and generally enjoy a better quality of life. This physical vitality often translates into a more active and satisfying sexual relationship, strengthening emotional bonds.

Conversely, poor physical health can become a point of strain. For instance, chronic illness or temporary health issues can limit activities and create stress, potentially leading to emotional distance or resentment. This is why maintaining a balanced diet, regular exercise, and adequate sleep are not just individual priorities but collective ones in the context of a healthy relationship.

Mental health plays an equally crucial role. Emotional well-being allows you to engage in meaningful communication, manage conflict effectively, and be a supportive partner. On the other hand, poor mental health can lead to a range of relationship problems, from communication breakdowns to severe emotional issues like depression or anxiety disorders, which can significantly affect both partners. It's not uncommon for relationships to suffer when one partner is experiencing mental health problems, as this often leads to emotional withdrawal, decreased intimacy, and increased tension.

Furthermore, taking care of your mental health often involves self-awareness and emotional intelligence. Understanding your emotional triggers and behavioural patterns can help you navigate relationship challenges more effectively. It also equips you to better understand your partner's emotional needs and responses, making for a more empathetic and supportive relationship. It might involve practices like mindfulness, counselling, or even medication for some individuals.

Both physical and mental health are interconnected in contributing to a person's overall sense of well-being. When you're feeling physically and emotionally good, you're more likely to be a patient, understanding, and loving partner. This creates a nurturing environment where both partners can thrive, and the relationship can flourish. Therefore, taking care of your physical and mental health is not just an act of self-love but also a crucial investment in the health and longevity of your relationship.

Grooming

The importance of grooming in a relationship extends beyond mere physical appearance or vanity. Grooming practices reflect your self-respect and, by extension, your respect for your partner and the relationship. When you take the time to maintain your personal hygiene and appearance, it signals that you value yourself and, consequently, that you value the relationship you're in. It shows that you care enough to present yourself well, not just for the outside world but especially for your partner, who is arguably the most significant person in your life.

Furthermore, grooming and taking care of oneself contribute to maintaining the initial physical attraction that often serves as the catalyst for romantic relationships. In the long term, sustaining this attraction

Addressing Needs, Wants, & Desires

can be vital for maintaining the overall health and satisfaction within the relationship. Physical attraction isn't solely about superficial looks; it also involves the effort and intentionality behind maintaining those looks. When someone shows that they are willing to make an effort to look good, it often reignites the initial spark that fueled the relationship's early days.

Good grooming habits also have a psychological impact. Feeling good about how you look boosts your self-esteem and confidence, which can positively affect how you interact with your partner. Confidence is often found to be an attractive quality, so this can add another layer of depth to your relationship. On a more practical level, good grooming can signify that you are organized and responsible, which can contribute to a more harmonious domestic life.

However, it's crucial to note that grooming is just one facet of a complex relationship and should be balanced with emotional connection, shared values, and mutual respect. It should not become an obsessive focus but rather be integrated into a holistic approach to maintaining a healthy relationship. The ultimate goal is to create an environment where both partners feel appreciated and valued emotionally and physically.

Good grooming habits are about more than just looking good; they're about feeling good, showing respect for yourself and your partner, and contributing to a holistic sense of well-being and mutual satisfaction within the relationship.

Culture

Building a culture within a relationship is a nuanced process beyond just spending time together or having shared interests. It involves consciously creating a shared set of values, expectations, and rituals that both partners agree upon and actively engage in. This collective "culture" essentially serves as the relationship's backbone, offering a consistent framework that guides how both partners interact with each other, make decisions, and handle conflicts or challenges. It can be likened to the culture within a company or organization, where established norms and values shape the behaviour and attitudes of its members.

For instance, some couples may prioritize open communication and make it a point to have a weekly "check-in" to discuss their feelings, concerns, or future plans. Others may value adventure and spontaneity, adopting a ritual of planning surprise getaways or outings for each other. There might be couples who share a deep spiritual connection, incorporating rituals or practices that nourish this aspect of their relationship. These can range from simple daily prayers together to attending religious services or engaging in spiritual study as a pair.

Creating a solid relationship culture also often involves setting mutual goals and expectations. This could relate to anything from financial planning and career goals to family planning or lifestyle choices like health and wellness routines. Aligning these aspects ensures that both partners are on the same page and fosters a sense of shared purpose and direction, making the relationship more resilient in the face of challenges.

Additionally, a robust relationship culture often incorporates mechanisms for conflict resolution. Since disagreements are inevitable in any relationship, having a pre-established, mutually agreed-upon approach to resolving conflicts can be invaluable. Whether it's a commitment to never go to bed angry or a promise to seek external mediation for more significant issues, these "cultural norms" can make navigating rough patches much smoother.

It's worth noting that a relationship's culture is not a static entity but rather a dynamic one that can evolve over time as both partners grow and change. As such, it's crucial to regularly revisit and potentially revise the "cultural norms" that you've established, ensuring they continue to serve the relationship effectively.

Addressing Needs, Wants, & Desires
Intimacy with Children in the Home

Maintaining intimacy in a relationship when children are in the home presents a unique set of challenges but is crucial for the long-term health and happiness of the partnership. The arrival of children often introduces a seismic shift in a couple's lifestyle, priorities, and daily routines. The time and energy that were once devoted primarily to each other may suddenly be redirected toward childcare, creating a potential emotional gap between partners. This change doesn't mean that intimacy should fall by the wayside; instead, it indicates a need for creative solutions to sustain the emotional and physical closeness that forms the bedrock of a healthy relationship.

One common strategy for maintaining intimacy is to schedule regular "date nights" or one-on-one time away from parental responsibilities. It may include getting a hotel room once a month or a weekend away without the children. While this may seem artificial or forced, setting aside dedicated time for each other can serve as a critical reminder of your relationship's importance. This doesn't always have to be a night out; it could be as simple as watching a movie together after the kids have gone to bed or sharing a quiet morning coffee before the day's chaos begins. The key is to create spaces where you can focus solely on each other, even if it's just for a short period.

Another approach to maintaining intimacy involves seizing brief moments of affection throughout the day. A hug, a kiss, or even a loving glance can go a long way in reinforcing emotional bonds. These small gestures serve as mini-affirmations of your love and commitment, offering a sense of continuity and emotional security amid the challenges of parenting.

Open and honest communication is also crucial in preserving intimacy. Parenting can be overwhelming, leading to stress and fatigue that might inadvertently get directed at your partner. Being transparent about your feelings, needs, and desires prevents misunderstandings and fosters emotional closeness. It's essential to discuss any frustrations or resentments as they arise rather than allowing them to fester and potentially lead to more significant issues.

Some couples also find it beneficial to involve children in practices that promote family closeness, which, in turn, can strengthen the parental relationship. For instance, regular family dinners or outings can offer a sense of unity and shared purpose that positively impacts the couple's relationship.

Maintaining intimacy with children in the home requires proactive efforts from both partners. Through planned quality time, daily moments of affection, and transparent communication, couples can navigate the complexities of parenthood without sacrificing the intimacy that sustains their relationship. This endeavour is about preserving the romantic relationship and modelling a healthy partnership for the children.

Tools to Kissing Breakups Goodbye

1. **Open Communication**: Open, honest, and frequent communication is the cornerstone of any strong relationship. This involves sharing your thoughts, feelings, and concerns and actively listening to your partner's perspective. Open communication allows for a deeper understanding of each other's needs, aspirations, and emotional states, fostering empathy and closeness. Regularly discussing feelings, expectations, and concerns creates an environment where misunderstandings are less likely to escalate into major conflicts.
2. **Quality Time**: Spending quality time together is not just about physical proximity but about emotional engagement. Whether it's a regular date night, a weekend getaway, or simply a few moments of undivided attention each day, these instances of quality time reinforce the emotional bonds between you and your partner. They act as a reminder of why you chose each other in the first place and help maintain a level of intimacy and

connection that can easily get lost in the hustle and bustle of daily life.

3. **Emotional Intelligence**: Emotional intelligence refers to the ability to understand, interpret, and manage emotions—both your own and those of people around you. In the context of a relationship, emotional intelligence enables you to recognize when your partner might be stressed, anxious, or in need of support, even if they haven't explicitly stated it. It also helps you manage your emotional responses in a way that considers your partner's feelings, thereby reducing unnecessary conflicts and misunderstandings.

4. **Conflict Resolution**: Every relationship faces disagreements and conflicts, but what distinguishes successful relationships from unsuccessful ones is the ability to resolve these conflicts in a healthy and respectful manner. This involves active listening, empathy, and sometimes even compromise. Learning techniques for effective conflict resolution can prevent minor disagreements from snowballing into significant issues that could threaten the relationship's stability.

5. **Professional Help**: Sometimes, despite best efforts, couples encounter issues they find difficult to resolve independently. In such cases, seeking the guidance of a qualified therapist or counsellor can provide valuable insights into the relationship's dynamics and offer strategies for improvement. Far from being a sign of failure, taking this step demonstrates a willingness to invest in the relationship's longevity and quality.

Breakups are often the result of neglected issues or unmet needs. By actively addressing these aspects and continually investing in the relationship, you significantly reduce the chances of reaching the point of separation. Each partner's commitment to mutual growth and happiness is often the best preventive measure against breakups.

THE *FOUR* **QUADRANTS**

Navigating the labyrinthine landscape of romantic relationships often feels like a complex task involving various emotional, intellectual, and practical dimensions. At different junctures in our romantic connections, we find ourselves playing diverse roles—sometimes a friend, sometimes a lover, and often, a life partner. This multiplicity of roles can be invigorating and challenging, requiring us to adapt and grow continually. Recognizing these varied facets and understanding how to nourish each one can be the key to sustaining a prosperous, fulfilling relationship over the long term.

It's no small feat to juggle these different aspects effectively. Each role we play in our romantic relationship is like a separate quadrant in the cartography of love, each with its unique terrain, climate, and navigational requirements. The concept of "The Four Quadrants" serves as a valuable framework for dissecting the complexity of romantic relationships into more manageable parts. By examining each quadrant—Friendship, Relationship, Partnership, and Companionship—we can gain valuable insights into what makes relationships flourish or flounder.

Addressing Needs, Wants, & Desires

The Friendship quadrant is often where it all begins. It forms the bedrock of emotional connection and mutual respect, qualities that sustain the relationship during turbulent times. Then there's the Relationship quadrant, which incorporates friendship and non-sexual intimacy, yet romantic. This is the level of adding a layer of non-physical intimacy yet holds an emotional depth beyond platonic friendship. Partnership, the third quadrant, brings shared responsibilities and life goals, offering a pragmatic lens through which to view the relationship. It's the level of marriage or common-law relationship, where sex and intimacy hold an emotional bond that goes beyond the friendship and relationship level. It's the level where emotional glue is produced through intimacy and sex. Learning each other's weaknesses and strengths, collaborating, compromising and complementing each other. It's the level with which a family is developed; children and grandchildren come into your world. Finally comes the companionship level, the growth of two people on the road to retirement. They have invested their lives with each other and now can live it with their children, grandchildren, and great-grandchildren. There is a significant emotional hold on everything, as the relationship has matured by this stage and has been through the tests of time. It's when both people can embrace each other and watch the sunset together, sitting closely in each other's arms.

Understanding these quadrants is not merely an academic exercise; it has practical implications. For instance, issues often arise in relationships when one quadrant is neglected at the expense of others. A relationship might have a robust Friendship quadrant but lack Partnership, leading to emotional closeness but practical disarray. Alternatively, a strong Partnership quadrant coupled with a weak Relationship quadrant might result in a functional but emotionally unsatisfying connection. To build a well-rounded, fulfilling relationship, it's crucial to invest in all four quadrants, each of which contributes uniquely to the overall health and happiness of the partnership.

THE FOUR QUADRANTS

Exploring the unique characteristics and roles in the relationship quadrants is essential. The practical tools to nourish each quadrant enhance the overall quality and longevity of the relationship. Consider how each quadrant manifests in your relationship and how you might strengthen each for a more fulfilling, long-lasting connection.

Friendship

Friendship is often considered the bedrock upon which many successful romantic relationships are built, and it remains a vital component throughout the life of the relationship. At its core, friendship embodies a mutual bond of affection, trust, and respect between individuals. This bond is a safe space where both parties can openly share their thoughts, feelings, and concerns without fearing judgment or ridicule. In essence, friends are emotional confidants who provide a sense of belonging and community, often acting as a sounding board for ideas or a shoulder to lean on during challenging times.

In the context of a romantic relationship, the importance of maintaining a solid friendship with your partner cannot be overstated. When you are friends with your partner, the relationship gains an additional layer of emotional intimacy that transcends the physical or romantic aspects. This friendship-based emotional closeness serves as a stabilizing force, particularly when the relationship faces challenges or periods of uncertainty. It provides a reservoir of goodwill and shared history that can make resolving conflicts easier and less fraught. Furthermore, friendship fosters an environment of mutual support, enabling each partner to pursue personal growth and individual goals while maintaining a solid relational bond.

The friendship aspect of a romantic relationship often involves shared interests and activities that both partners enjoy. Participating in these shared activities creates lasting memories and strengthens the emotional connection between partners. Whether watching a favourite TV show together, hiking on weekends, or cooking a meal, these joint activities contribute to a sense of partnership and mutual enjoyment that can significantly enrich the relationship.

Moreover, friendship within a romantic relationship often evolves like any other friendship. It requires continuous investment in time, emotional availability, and active interest in your partner's well-being. Regular check-ins, open communication about emotional needs, and the occasional surprise or thoughtful gesture can go a long way in keeping the friendship aspect of a romantic relationship vibrant and fulfilling.

Therefore, the friendship quadrant of a relationship is not merely a starting point or a convenient category; it's an ongoing, evolving aspect that requires attention and care. It's a space where mutual respect thrives, vulnerabilities are shared, and both partners can be their authentic selves without fear of judgment. By understanding the nuances of friendship and actively nurturing this aspect, you enhance not only the emotional richness of your relationship but also its resilience and longevity.

Relationship

In the context of romantic involvement, a relationship is a multifaceted bond that goes significantly beyond the parameters of friendship. It encompasses a deep emotional connection, non-physical intimacy, and often a vision for a shared future. While friendships generally involve emotional support and common interests, relationships elevate these elements by adding multiple layers of complexity, such as emotional interdependence and often intertwined financial resources.

In a relationship, a heightened level of commitment typically includes expectations about exclusivity, long-term intentions, and a more profound form of emotional and physical closeness. Partners in a romantic relationship often navigate shared responsibilities ranging from everyday tasks like cooking and cleaning to more substantial commitment discussions like marriage or cohabitation. These responsibilities often require a harmonious blend of effective communication, shared values, and mutual respect.

Moreover, a romantic relationship may also involve shared long-term goals, such as building a family, purchasing a home, or planning retirement. These shared objectives often serve as milestones that mark the relationship's progression and provide both partners with a sense of purpose and direction. Achieving these goals usually necessitates a cooperative effort involving both emotional and practical contributions from both parties.

Additionally, romantic relationships often involve an element of vulnerability that goes beyond what is commonly shared in friendships. This vulnerability comes from the emotional investment and the interconnected lives that relationships foster. Partners may share joys and successes, fears, insecurities, and challenges. The ability to be vulnerable and the trust that vulnerability fosters can strengthen the emotional bonds between partners, making the relationship more resilient and enriching.

This multifaceted nature of romantic relationships makes them both rewarding and challenging. They require a continuous investment of time, emotional energy, and, often, financial resources. Both partners must be attuned to each other's needs, willing to make sacrifices, and committed to constructively resolving conflicts. However, the payoff for this investment is a profoundly fulfilling connection that offers emotional support, personal growth opportunities, and the joy and comfort of shared life experiences.

Partnership

In the context of a romantic relationship, the term "partnership" takes on a meaning that transcends the emotional and interpersonal dynamics commonly associated with love or friendship. A partnership implies a functional, practical interdependence often anchored in shared responsibilities and goals. This is not just about emotional support; it's about creating a life together in a tangible sense. This is the level when

Addressing Needs, Wants, & Desires

two people decide to join their hearts together. They get married or cohabitate. They share full responsibility, enjoy the privilege of being sexually intimate with each other and start a life that may evolve into a family.

The partnership aspect of a romantic relationship is often legally formalized in marriages or civil unions, but it exists in many committed relationships regardless of legal status. It's the part of the relationship that requires ongoing negotiation, clear communication, and sometimes even formal agreements. Each partner has to be willing to make compromises and sometimes sacrifice individual wants or needs for the good of the partnership.

In a partnership, each individual contributes to the relationship in a way that benefits the collective unit. This could involve financial planning, where both parties actively engage in budgeting, saving, and investing for their shared future. It could also extend to co-parenting, where both partners are equally involved in raising children, from attending parent-teacher meetings to sharing in the daily tasks of childcare. Beyond finances and family, partnerships also often involve shared ownership or investment in property, joint decision-making about relocating for job opportunities, and even mundane day-to-day tasks like grocery shopping or household chores.

Notably, a healthy partnership is characterized by a balanced distribution of responsibilities. It's not about one person taking on all the burdens while the other coasts along; it's about both partners sharing the load equitably. This balance doesn't necessarily have to mean a 50-50 split in every task or responsibility; instead, it's about each partner contributing according to their abilities, resources, and expertise. For instance, if one partner is better at handling finances, they might take on the primary role of managing the household budget. In contrast, the other might take charge of different aspects like planning family activities or home maintenance.

A shared vision for the future is another vital component of a successful partnership. Both partners must be aligned in their long-term

THE FOUR QUADRANTS

goals, whether buying a home, planning for retirement, or deciding not to have children. This shared vision is a guiding star for the relationship, helping both partners make decisions that move them closer to these mutual goals.

The partnership quadrant of a relationship is a complex, multifaceted domain that involves much more than love or affection. It requires skills like effective communication, financial planning, conflict resolution and trial and error. The practical, logistical aspect of a relationship allows the emotional and romantic parts to flourish, providing a stable foundation upon which the rest of the relationship can be built.

Companionship

Companionship in the context of a romantic relationship holds a nuanced and multi-dimensional role, embodying a deep emotional closeness that transcends the need for constant interaction or even romantic or sexual engagement in retirement life. It represents the comfort, peace, and emotional stability that arise from being with someone you deeply care about where you retire and enjoy the fruits of your labour. This companionship is often the emotional glue that holds long-term relationships together, providing a consistent sense of togetherness even when life's challenges become overwhelming.

In mature relationships, companionship often manifests as a kind of emotional sanctuary. In this safe space, both partners can let down their guard and be their most authentic selves without fear of judgment. Through their years of being together, both partners have learned each other's strengths and weaknesses. They have learned to accept each other without trying to shape or control the parent or be the boss over each other. It's the warmth you feel when sitting silently together watching a sunset, the contentment from a shared laugh, or the comfort in knowing someone is there for you, even if words are not exchanged.

Addressing Needs, Wants, & Desires

Companionship is what often remains when the initial phases of physical attraction and infatuation have evolved. It's the everyday presence and the gentle constancy of someone who has become deeply embedded in the texture of your life. Importantly, companionship can serve as an antidote to loneliness and emotional isolation, providing a sense of belonging and community within the microcosm of the relationship itself.

Moreover, the value of companionship often becomes increasingly evident as a relationship endures various life phases. During times of crisis, upheaval, or significant life changes, the mere presence of a reliable companion can provide a stabilizing influence. Conversely, companionship amplifies happiness in celebration and joy by giving someone to share and multiply the good times with.

In essence, companionship serves as both a refuge from life's challenges and a repository for shared memories and experiences. It enriches the relationship by adding a layer of emotional depth that is less about excitement and novelty and more about enduring love and mutual respect. Consequently, nurturing this form of emotional closeness can significantly contribute to the overall health and longevity of the relationship.

Couples can enjoy their retirement, children, grandchildren, great-grandchildren and some of their great-grandchildren. They can travel, cruise, and enjoy themselves before leaving this planet. They create memorable moments for those they love and share the wisdom they gained from their journey together.

Tools to Have a Healthy, Long-Lasting Relationship

1. **Emotional Availability**: Being emotionally present and open with your partner fosters a deeper connection.
2. **Mutual Respect**: Treating each other with dignity and valuing each other's opinions form the basis of a healthy relationship.
3. **Effective Communication**: Expressing your needs, desires, and concerns clearly and openly is crucial for relationship longevity.

THE FOUR QUADRANTS

4. **Shared Goals and Values**: A mutual understanding of life goals and values can provide a roadmap for the relationship's future.
5. **Quality Time**: Spend time together regularly, engaging in activities that both enjoy, to strengthen emotional bonds.
6. **Conflict Resolution Skills**: Learn how to resolve disagreements amicably and constructively.
7. **Financial Transparency**: Open and honest discussions about financial expectations and responsibilities can prevent misunderstandings later.
8. **Individual Growth**: Support each other's personal and professional growth to ensure the relationship evolves and matures.
9. **Professional Counseling**: Sometimes, professional guidance is necessary to navigate complex emotional or relational issues effectively.
10. **Continuous Learning**: Stay updated with each other's changing preferences, career advancements, and emotional needs to ensure the relationship adapts and grows.
11. **Trust Building**: Regular acts of kindness, reliability, and openness can significantly enhance the trust between you and your partner.

Understanding these four quadrants—Friendship, Relationship, Partnership, and Companionship—provides a comprehensive view of what a romantic relationship can entail. Each quadrant serves a unique purpose and satisfies different emotional and practical needs. Fostering each quadrant's growth and balance is critical to a successful, long-lasting relationship. By applying the appropriate tools and practices, you can cultivate a relationship that thrives on multiple levels, offering emotional warmth, practical support, deep intimacy, and a shared journey through life.

BUILDING CONFIDENCE

Building confidence within a relationship is akin to fortifying a structure that both parties inhabit. Just as a house needs a solid foundation to withstand external forces, a relationship requires a robust sense of confidence to navigate the challenges and complexities of shared life. This chapter is designed to explore the multiple facets of instilling and nurturing confidence within the context of a romantic partnership. Confidence is not merely an individual attribute but a collective asset that strengthens the relationship's integrity and resilience. It is a critical ingredient that enhances trust, fosters emotional intimacy, and enables both partners to engage with each other authentically and vulnerably.

Confidence in a relationship starts with each partner's self-assurance but goes beyond encompassing a shared sense of reliability and mutual respect. It's the glue that binds commitments and expectations, the lens through which both parties view their shared experiences and the foundation upon which they build their future. In the absence of confidence, relationships can become breeding grounds for insecurity, mistrust, and emotional detachment. Contrarily, a confident relationship acts as a wellspring of emotional security, intellectual engagement, and mutual growth.

BUILDING CONFIDENCE

However, confidence is not a static quality; it's dynamic and responsive to the relationship's ever-changing circumstances. It's built over time through consistent actions, transparent communication, and the mutual fulfillment of promises and expectations. And like any other aspect of a relationship, it requires maintenance. Long-lasting relationships often go through phases that could shake their core confidence. These could range from personal setbacks like job loss or health issues to relational hurdles like conflicts or breaches of trust. In such times, the foundational confidence that partners have nurtured can serve as a stabilizing force, helping them navigate challenges effectively.

Confidence is also intrinsically linked to several other relationship dynamics, such as emotional support, communication, and the ability to resolve conflicts. A confident partner is more likely to express feelings openly, listen attentively, and engage in constructive problem-solving. Likewise, a confident relationship fosters an environment where both parties feel empowered to be their authentic selves without fear of judgment or ridicule. This sense of emotional safety, in turn, enhances other relationship attributes like intimacy, trust, and mutual respect.

This chapter explores how to build and maintain confidence in a relationship, focusing on practical strategies and emotional paradigms that can foster this essential quality. We'll delve into the dynamics of maximizing love and appreciation, discuss the importance of service and compromise, and offer tools that can help solidify your relationship's confidence foundation. As we navigate through the topics, the overarching goal remains the same: to equip you with the understanding and tools you need to build a relationship that is not just confident but also enriching, fulfilling, and resilient. Let's begin by discussing how and why bringing out the best in your relationship is essential.

Addressing Needs, Wants, & Desires

Pull Out the Best

Pulling out the best in a relationship is an ongoing, conscious endeavour that involves numerous facets of interaction between the partners. This process is vitally important for several reasons. Primarily, it establishes an environment where both individuals can achieve their fullest potential, not just within the bounds of the relationship but also in their personal and professional lives. Creating such an environment involves leveraging each person's strengths to compensate for the other's weaknesses, fostering mutual empowerment. For example, if one partner is particularly good at handling finances while the other excels in emotional intelligence, acknowledging and utilizing these strengths can provide a well-rounded approach to managing money and emotional well-being.

This intentional focus on drawing out the best creates a positive feedback loop. When one partner experiences personal growth and emotional satisfaction within the relationship, they become more motivated to contribute positively in return, benefiting the other partner and the relationship. This goes beyond mere transactional interactions and enters the realm of a deeply interconnected, mutually beneficial dynamic.

Furthermore, emphasizing the best aspects of each other and the relationship contributes to resilience. Every relationship faces challenges, from external pressures like job loss or health issues to internal conflicts like disagreements or emotional disconnection. A relationship built on a solid foundation of mutual respect, trust, and constructive engagement is better equipped to navigate these challenges successfully. It provides a form of emotional and psychological buoyancy that can help both partners weather the storms they may encounter.

Moreover, this focus on the best aspects serves as a powerful antidote to negativity and conflict. It's easy to become embroiled in what's going wrong in a relationship, especially during times of stress

BUILDING CONFIDENCE

or discord. By consciously choosing to focus on what's going well, you create an opportunity to shift the narrative and reframe the relationship in a more positive light. This can help defuse tension and create a pathway to resolving conflicts more constructively.

The ultimate goal is to create a nurturing, enriching environment where both individuals feel valued, respected, and inspired to grow. This requires ongoing effort, including regular communication to ensure that both partners are on the same page and a commitment to adapt and evolve as the relationship changes over time. It means investing time, emotional energy, and, when necessary, material resources to ensure that the relationship remains a source of joy, support, and personal fulfillment for both parties.

Dominate a Relationship with Love

Dominating a relationship with love is a concept that may initially sound contradictory, but in essence, it's about letting love be the guiding principle in all facets of the relationship. This approach shifts the focus away from power dynamics and control, redirecting it towards mutual respect, care, and emotional support. When love dominates the relationship, decisions are made with consideration for both individuals involved rather than for selfish or unilateral reasons.

In a relationship dominated by love, each action, conversation, and decision is steeped in kindness and understanding. This sets the stage for a culture of empathy, where each partner endeavours to understand the other's point of view, even when disagreements arise. This doesn't mean that conflicts never occur or challenges never present themselves. Instead, it means that when such situations arise, they are addressed in a manner that is respectful and loving, aimed at finding a solution that honours both individuals.

Furthermore, in a love-dominated relationship, the emotional well-being of both partners is a priority. Acts of service, words of affirmation, and other love languages are occasional highlights and regular occurrences. These consistent expressions of love strengthen the emotional bonds between partners, making them feel secure and valued in the relationship.

When love is the dominant force, it also enables both individuals to be authentic, removing the masks often worn for societal approval or personal protection. Authenticity brings with it a level of intimacy and understanding that is hard to achieve otherwise. In such a nurturing environment, each person feels empowered to explore their potential, knowing they have their partner's emotional support and encouragement.

Moreover, a relationship dominated by love tends to be one where both partners are invested in mutual growth. Whether emotional, intellectual, or even spiritual growth, the focus remains on evolving as a unit. This collective growth not only enhances the quality of the relationship but also contributes to the personal development of each individual.

So, when discussing dominating a relationship with love, we create a relational environment where love is the primary motivator and influencer. In such a relationship, love dictates the rhythm, setting the tone for interactions and shaping the relationship narrative in an inclusive, nurturing, and deeply respectful way. This creates a virtuous cycle where love begets more love, continually strengthening the relationship and making it more resilient in the face of challenges.

Maximize Love in a Relationship

Maximizing love in a relationship is an ongoing, multifaceted endeavour involving much more than physical affection or verbal affirmations. It's about creating a nurturing emotional environment where both parties feel loved, respected, valued, and genuinely cared for. This type of emotional climate doesn't materialize spontaneously; it requires deliberate and continuous effort from both individuals involved.

BUILDING CONFIDENCE

One of the key components to maximizing love is active emotional presence. This means genuinely being there for your partner—mentally, emotionally, and physically. When you're emotionally present, you're not just physically near your partner but also mentally engaged in your interactions with them. You're not scrolling through your phone while having a conversation; instead, you're looking into their eyes, listening intently, and responding thoughtfully. Emotional presence conveys that you value your time with your partner, enhancing the feeling of being loved.

Another critical aspect is active participation in each other's lives. This extends beyond asking about your partner's day; it means being involved in their interests, supporting their endeavours, and showing up when it counts. Whether it's a work event that's important to them or a hobby they're passionate about, your active interest and support can go a long way in demonstrating your love.

Consistent acts of kindness, no matter how small, also contribute to maximizing love. Whether making your partner a cup of coffee in the morning or leaving a sweet note in their bag, these small acts accumulate over time to create a backdrop of warmth and affection. They serve as constant reminders of your love and make your partner feel cherished and valued in the relationship.

Appreciation and gratitude are also powerful tools for maximizing love. When you express appreciation for the things your partner does—whether it's big things like being a supportive partner or small things like doing household chores—you not only make them feel valued but also reinforce positive behaviour. Moreover, showing gratitude helps you focus on the positive aspects of your relationship, which can enhance your feelings of love and satisfaction.

Mutual growth is another vital area for maximizing love. Relationships, like individuals, need to grow to stay healthy. This means supporting each other's personal and professional growth, encouraging new experiences, and developing together as a couple. Whether it's

Addressing Needs, Wants, & Desires

picking up a new hobby together or setting mutual life goals, the act of growing together can deepen your emotional connection and enhance your love for one another.

Maximizing love in a relationship is a complex but rewarding endeavour that involves emotional presence, active participation, consistent acts of kindness, mutual appreciation, and shared growth. These elements work in concert to create a deep, meaningful emotional connection that can sustain and enrich the relationship over the long term.

Appreciation

Appreciation serves as a vital emotional nutrient in the ecosystem of a relationship. When individuals within a couple feel genuinely appreciated for who they are and what they contribute, the entire dynamic of their interaction shifts toward the positive. This sense of being valued stimulates a variety of beneficial behaviours and attitudes. For instance, you're more likely to show appreciation when you feel appreciated, creating a cycle of goodwill and positive reinforcement.

Appreciation can be seen as an emotional currency that builds a reservoir of goodwill. It helps buffer against the inevitable challenges and conflicts that arise in any relationship. When you feel appreciated, minor annoyances and setbacks are less likely to escalate into major issues. This emotional padding can be indispensable for navigating through more difficult periods in a relationship.

Furthermore, consistent appreciation nurtures a sense of security and emotional well-being. When you know your efforts are noticed and valued, you're more inclined to go that extra mile, not just in reciprocating affection but also in working through problems and disagreements constructively. On the other hand, feeling underappreciated can lead to resentment, often a precursor to more

BUILDING CONFIDENCE

severe relationship problems. Therefore, appreciation acts as both a preventive and a curative measure.

Moreover, showing appreciation often encourages a more mindful approach to the relationship. It requires you to pay attention, notice the small kindnesses and the grand gestures, and acknowledge them openly. This level of attentiveness can significantly deepen emotional intimacy, encouraging both partners to be present and engaged in their interactions.

Overall, showing and receiving appreciation enriches the relationship by enhancing emotional intimacy, reducing potential friction, and fostering a secure, loving environment. It's a simple yet profoundly effective way to fortify the relationship's emotional health over the long term.

Start a Gratitude Jar

Incorporating a gratitude jar into your relationship is a powerful, tangible exercise in mindfulness and appreciation. The very act of writing down what you're thankful for shifts your focus away from what might be lacking or imperfect in your relationship to what is enriching and positive. Over time, these collected notes of gratitude act as a reservoir of positivity that can be incredibly uplifting during challenging times.

The practice of filling a gratitude jar encourages a culture of appreciation and acknowledgment within the relationship. Each note serves as a concrete acknowledgment of love, kindness, or thoughtful action, validating each partner's efforts to nurture the relationship. This ongoing validation enhances the emotional well-being of both partners, reinforcing the efforts and intentions behind actions that might otherwise go unnoticed.

Additionally, the gratitude jar can serve as a valuable tool for reflection. During moments of conflict or strain, revisiting the notes can provide a broader perspective, reminding both partners of their shared happiness and mutual respect. It is a repository of positive memories and affirmations that can help balance the scales when the relationship goes through inevitable ups and downs.

Creating a gratitude jar also fosters a shared ritual that enhances relationship intimacy. The act of jointly contributing to the jar encourages a collective focus on the positive aspects of your relationship, reinforcing mutual goals of fostering appreciation and emotional connection. It becomes a mutually beneficial exercise that not only uplifts individual spirits but also fortifies the emotional foundations of the relationship itself.

Starting a gratitude jar can be seen as an investment in the emotional health of your relationship. This simple yet powerful tool can amplify positive interactions, mitigate the impact of negative experiences, and serve as a constant reminder of the love, respect, and appreciation that both partners bring into the relationship.

Be an Asset

Being an asset in a relationship extends far beyond financial contributions or fulfilling traditional roles; it's about enriching the relationship in meaningful ways that promote growth, stability, and happiness. This multifaceted concept covers emotional, intellectual, and even spiritual dimensions. Emotional support, for instance, is invaluable. Whether providing a listening ear after a tough day or offering constructive advice during decision-making, your emotional presence can be a pillar of strength for your partner. Similarly, your ability to deal with conflicts maturely, to communicate openly, and to show empathy can make you an asset because these qualities contribute to a healthier, more harmonious relationship.

Being an asset also means bringing your unique skills, talents, and perspectives into the relationship. These could range from practical skills like budget management or cooking to intellectual and creative abilities that can be a source of inspiration and growth for both parties. Sharing responsibilities in a way that leverages each partner's strengths and compensates for their weaknesses can also make you an invaluable asset in the relationship.

Additionally, being an asset involves contributing to a shared future vision. Whether it's co-building a home, planning vacations, or strategizing for mutual career growth, your ability to contribute positively to these long-term plans makes you indispensable and adds layers of depth and purpose to the relationship. It demonstrates your commitment and signals to your partner that you're invested in not just the present but also the future of the relationship.

Moreover, being an asset isn't just about what you bring into the relationship; it's also about how adaptable and flexible you are. Relationships aren't static; they evolve, facing various challenges and phases. Your ability to adapt, learn, and grow with your partner, especially during trying times, is an invaluable asset that can significantly impact the relationship's longevity and quality.

In essence, being an asset in a relationship is about being a positive, enriching influence in your partner's life. It's about adding value in various tangible and intangible forms to create a fulfilling, mutually beneficial relationship. This enriches the relationship and each individual's personal life, elevating the partnership to a source of joy, support, and personal growth.

Avoid Pointing Fingers

Avoiding the blame game and refraining from pointing fingers during conflicts is critical to sustaining a healthy and mature relationship. The tendency to blame is often a defensive mechanism, a way to protect oneself from criticism or to divert attention away from one's shortcomings. However, this approach is counterproductive and can escalate conflicts rather than resolve them. Instead of playing the blame game, the focus should shift towards understanding the root cause of the issue and finding a collaborative solution. This problem-solving mindset is more constructive and helps to maintain an atmosphere of mutual respect and understanding. It also fosters emotional safety, as both partners feel heard and valued rather than attacked or marginalized.

Active listening is critical to shift from a blame-oriented approach to a problem-solving one successfully. It involves genuinely hearing what your partner is saying without immediately formulating a counter-argument, which can be a natural impulse in heated moments. Active listening is aided by repeating what you've heard, asking clarifying questions, and resisting the urge to interrupt. It's also essential to use "I" statements to express how you feel and what you need rather than accusing your partner of causing your emotional state. For instance, saying, "I felt hurt when you forgot our anniversary," is more constructive and less accusatory than saying, "You hurt me by forgetting our anniversary."

Additionally, it's crucial to remember that you and your partner are a team. The problem you're facing is a mutual challenge to be solved together, not a battleground for proving who's right or wrong. Approaching conflicts with this team mindset often makes it easier to avoid pointing fingers and instead focus on how to resolve the issue at hand.

By adopting these strategies, you can avoid the destructive cycle of blame and counter-blame, moving instead toward more constructive, respectful, and ultimately more effective problem-solving. This de-escalates conflicts and strengthens the relationship by building a culture of mutual respect, understanding, and collaborative problem-solving.

Compromise

The concept of compromise in a romantic relationship often carries with it a sense of mutual adjustment and shared sacrifice for the greater good of the partnership. While the term itself might imply a giving up of something, in the context of a healthy relationship, compromise is less about loss and more about gain. It's about creating a balanced relational ecosystem where both individuals' needs, desires, and aspirations are acknowledged and accommodated to the greatest extent possible.

In a well-balanced relationship, compromise serves as a tool for bridging gaps—whether they are gaps in communication, differences in lifestyle choices, or divergent future plans. When both individuals approach compromise with an attitude of fairness and mutual respect, the act becomes an exercise of empathy and understanding. It shifts the focus from 'I versus you' to 'us,' fostering a collective identity that can weather challenges more effectively than two isolated individuals could.

However, it's essential to note that compromise should never be one-sided or coerced, as that can lead to feelings of resentment or exploitation. It should not involve sacrificing core values or critical personal needs. Instead, successful compromise involves open dialogue to explore the range of options available and to understand the potential consequences of various choices. This dialogue enables both partners to find a middle ground that respects both parties' core needs and values.

Moreover, compromise is often not a one-time event but an ongoing process. As the relationship matures and circumstances change, what seemed like a fair compromise at one point may need reevaluation and adjustment. Therefore, the willingness to revisit past agreements and make necessary changes is also essential to healthy compromise.

When carried out thoughtfully and respectfully, compromise enriches the relationship by incorporating the perspectives and needs of both individuals. It functions as a mechanism for conflict resolution, promotes shared decision-making, and ultimately strengthens the emotional bonds between partners. It's a vital skill that enables couples to navigate the complexities of life together, enhancing both the durability and the quality of the relationship.

Addressing Needs, Wants, & Desires

Serving

In the context of a romantic relationship, the concept of serving extends far beyond mere subservience or the fulfillment of duties. Instead, serving your partner means being actively engaged in nurturing their well-being, both emotional and physical, sometimes even putting their needs on an equal footing with, or above, your own. Importantly, this is not about sacrificing your individuality, self-respect, or your own needs but about demonstrating a kind of attentiveness and care that fosters a mutual culture of respect, support, and love.

Serving involves various actions and behaviours, ranging from simple acts of kindness, like making a cup of coffee in the morning, to more substantial forms of support, such as emotional availability during challenging times. It could mean taking the time to understand your partner's point of view during a disagreement rather than focusing solely on your perspective. Serving can also extend to acts of emotional vulnerability—opening up about your fears and insecurities in a way that invites your partner to do the same.

Moreover, serving your partner in a relationship often has a reciprocal effect. When one person feels genuinely cared for and supported, they are more likely to reciprocate, thereby creating a cycle of positive engagement. This ongoing exchange enhances the overall emotional climate of the relationship, making both individuals more willing and able to invest in its growth and longevity.

In essence, serving within a relationship is not just about the individual's acts but about adopting a mindset of proactive love and care. It's about committing to your partner's well-being as a path to mutual happiness. This dedication doesn't just happen; it's cultivated intentionally over time and becomes a cornerstone of a healthy, thriving relationship.

BUILDING CONFIDENCE

Love Infinitely

Loving infinitely in a relationship is an ambitious but profoundly rewarding endeavour that extends beyond mere emotional or physical attraction. It's a form of love not limited by time, circumstance, or superficial attributes. This kind of infinite love is characterized by an unyielding commitment to the relationship and an unwavering desire to cultivate mutual happiness and well-being. To love infinitely, you must engage in a perpetual cycle of emotional investment, open communication, and mutual growth.

This concept of infinite love is not static; it's dynamic and requires ongoing effort from both parties. It involves continually adapting to each other's needs, wishes, and life circumstances. The focus is not just on immediate emotional or physical satisfaction but also on fostering a lasting bond that can withstand various challenges, whether personal struggles, external pressures, or changes over time.

To love infinitely is to make a conscious daily choice to prioritize the relationship and act in ways that nourish its growth. It's about being present, not just physically but emotionally and mentally, for your partner. It's about showing kindness and understanding, even when faced with disagreements or difficulties. It's about celebrating successes together and facing hardships hand in hand.

Infinite love also encompasses the ability to forgive and to look beyond imperfections, understanding that every individual is a work in progress. It's not about idealizing your partner but about accepting them wholeheartedly, flaws and all, and loving them not just for who they are but for who they can become.

Such a form of love is not achieved overnight. It's built on a foundation of shared experiences, mutual respect, and a deep understanding of each other's inner worlds. It's reinforced by the joy derived from giving and receiving love unconditionally and the sense of security and belonging that comes from being in a committed relationship.

To love infinitely is to commit to nurturing, understanding, and growing with your partner. It's about creating a relationship that serves as both a sanctuary and a source of inspiration. This relationship not only withstands the test of time but continually grows stronger with each passing moment.

Tools to Build Confidence

1. **Positive Affirmations**: Regularly affirming each other's worth can significantly boost confidence within the relationship.
2. **Mutual Goals**: Setting and achieving goals together enhances self-efficacy and builds collective confidence.
3. **Active Listening**: Listening attentively can validate your partner's feelings and increase emotional security.
4. **Transparency**: Honest and open communication removes ambiguity, leading to a more secure and confident relationship dynamic.
5. **Personal Growth**: Encouraging each other's personal and professional development can enhance individual confidence levels, contributing to a more robust relationship.
6. **Feedback Mechanism**: Constructive feedback helps in self-improvement and thus boosts confidence.

Confidence within a relationship not only contributes to the individual self-esteem of each partner but also enhances the overall quality of the relationship. A confident relationship is more resilient, fulfilling, and equipped to navigate the complexities and challenges that inevitably arise. Therefore, building and maintaining confidence is critical for a long-lasting, satisfying relationship.

BUILDING CONFIDENCE

CONCLUSION

Relationships are often referred to as one of life's most rewarding yet challenging pursuits. They involve an intricate interplay of emotions, communication, compromise, and personal growth. This guide invites you to embark on a transformative journey of discovery—learning not only what it takes to cultivate healthy, meaningful relationships but also how to bring your best self to them.

From the foundational chapters, the exploration of **Purpose and Value** sets the tone for understanding relationships beyond surface-level desires. It delves into the profound purpose of relationships, clarifying that they are not solely about meeting individual needs but about creating something mutually enriching. The discussions on recognizing worth, self-value, and the contributions of skills and experiences highlight how personal growth and acknowledgment of one's own potential can elevate any connection.

CONCLUSION

The section on **Investment** emphasizes the importance of viewing relationships as meaningful endeavors requiring thoughtful effort. By comparing relationships to a business partnership, the chapters teach us the value of investing time, energy, and resources into nurturing love. The tools provided ensure that such investments bring about fruitful outcomes, teaching us to continuously grow and adapt in ways that enrich relationships.

The core of the book lies in **Understanding**—a theme that permeates every chapter. By learning about each other's strengths, addressing insecurities, accepting imperfections, and navigating mental health challenges, you can build the foundations for a relationship steeped in empathy and mutual respect. The chapters here provide tools for uncovering deeper insights into your partner's behaviors and perspectives, empowering you to create a safe and supportive environment for growth.

For those seeking to overcome challenges, the section on **Conflict Resolutions** offers invaluable strategies. It tackles topics such as addressing unresolved issues, navigating difficult conversations, and overcoming environments of tension or mistrust. Whether addressing gaslighting or discussing sensitive subjects like addiction, the tools and techniques offered promote honest communication and pave the way for healing.

As we delve into **Parenting Each Other**, the chapters explore the dynamics of nurturing and support within relationships. While fostering growth is essential, the guide reminds us to avoid behaviors like controlling or putting one another down, focusing instead on uplifting and empowering our partner. It encourages healthy boundaries and collaboration, ensuring the relationship remains balanced and equitable.

The practical chapters on **Cultivating Relationships** offer actionable advice for sustaining long-term connections. From nurturing affection and intimacy to fostering effective communication and trust,

Addressing Needs, Wants, & Desires

these chapters create a roadmap for building relationships that withstand life's ups and downs. The emphasis on love languages and bathing relationships with positive "fertilizers" reminds us that consistent care and attention are vital for keeping love alive.

The exploration of **Friendship, Partnership, and Companionship** rounds out the relational journey, shedding light on the multifaceted nature of human connections. These chapters affirm that relationships are not simply romantic partnerships—they encompass meaningful friendships and shared experiences that form the foundation of a life well-lived. The tools provided ensure that each relational aspect is nurtured, creating a holistic and fulfilling life with those who matter most.

Finally, the section on **Building Confidence** empowers you to bring your best self to your relationships. From fostering appreciation and practicing gratitude to compromising and serving each other, the tools provided reinforce the idea that relationships are not about perfection but about authentic, loving effort. The act of loving infinitely becomes the cornerstone of every interaction, ensuring that your relationships radiate positivity and strength.

This book is more than a manual for relationship-building; it is a transformative tool designed to foster deeper connections, personal growth, and mutual fulfillment. Its chapters weave together insights that challenge conventional thinking, offering a comprehensive approach to relationships. Whether you are searching for love, deepening an existing connection, or striving to improve your relational skills for the future, the tools and wisdom shared throughout this book equip you to navigate the complexities of love with grace and confidence.

Relationships evolve as we do, presenting new challenges, opportunities, and ways to grow. As you implement the strategies and insights from this book, remember that the journey is just as important as the destination. With empathy, understanding, and intentionality, you

CONCLUSION

can cultivate relationships that are not only healthy and enduring but also deeply enriching for both you and your partner.

Embrace this journey wholeheartedly, knowing that every step is shaping the love you desire into a reality. With dedication, patience, and faith, the relationships you nurture today can become the foundation for a lifetime of connection, growth, and unwavering joy. Let this guide inspire you to cultivate love that is infinite, purposeful, and transformative. You hold the power to create lasting connections, and the journey ahead is filled with possibility!

www.ingramcontent.com/pod-product-compliance
Lightning Source LLC
Chambersburg PA
CBHW010448010526
44118CB00019B/2512